HOW DO WE KNOW
WHAT'S
INSIDE US?

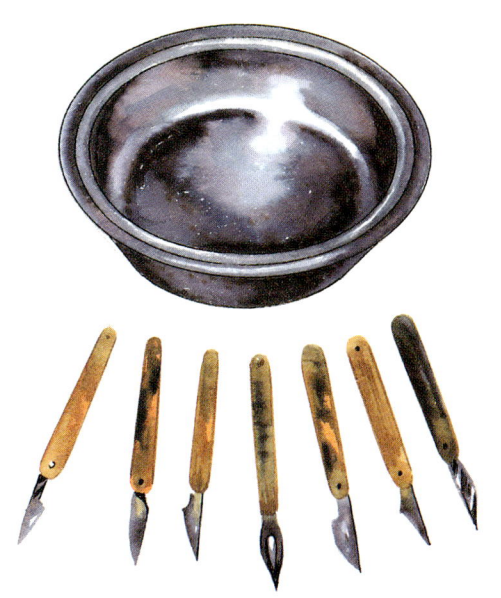

ANITA GANERI

RAINTREE
STECK-VAUGHN
P U B L I S H E R S
The Steck-Vaughn Company

Austin, Texas

© Copyright 1995, text, Steck-Vaughn Company

All rights reserved. No part of this book may be reproduced or utilized in any form or by any means, electronic or mechanical, including photocopying, recording, or by any information storage and retrieval system, without permission in writing from the Publisher. Inquiries should be addressed to: Copyright Permissions, Steck-Vaughn Company, P.O. Box 26015, Austin, TX 78755

Published by Raintree Steck-Vaughn Publishers, an imprint of Steck-Vaughn Company

Commissioning Editor: Thomas Keegan
Designer: Andrew Oliver
Editors: Kate Scarborough, Maurice J. Sabean
Illustrators: Victor Ambrus, Simone End, Roger Gorringe, Sandie Hill, Rodney Shackell, and Debra Woodward.

Library of Congress Cataloging-in-Publication Data
Ganeri, Anita, 1961–
What's inside us? / Anita Ganeri.
p. cm.—(How do we know)
Includes index.
ISBN 0-8114-3885-6
1. Human physiology—Juvenile literature. [1. Body, Human.
2. Human physiology.] I. Title. II. Series.
QP37.G34 1995
612—dc20
94-19406
CIP
AC

Picture Acknowledgements

The Bridgeman Art Library 30 bottom (Giraudon), 32; Mary Evans Picture Library 9, 10, 12 left, 15, 17, 18, 19, 28 top & bottom left, 30 top, 31, 34, 35, 38; Image Select 12 right, 23 top & middle; Science Photo Library 16 left (P Menzel), 23 bottom (W&D McIntyre), 28 middle (A B Dowsett) & bottom right (J-L Charmet), 33; Sporting Pictures UK Ltd 16 right; The Wellcome Centre Medical Photographic Library 6, 20

Printed and bound in Hong Kong

1 2 3 4 5 6 7 8 9 0 HK 99 98 97 96 95 94

The words in boldface type are explained in the glossary.

Contents

HOW DO WE KNOW

What We Are Made Of? 4
Why We Can Stand Up? 6
Muscles Help Us Move? 8
What Flows in Our Veins? 10
Blood Moves Through the Body? 12
There's Air in Our Lungs? 14
Why We Have to Eat? 16
What Controls Our Body? 18
What We Feel? 20
We See What We See? 22
Which Way Is Up? 24
What We Like to Eat? 26
Germs Make Us Sick? 28
How We Get Better? 30
What's Inside Us? 32
Where We Come From? 34
About Hormones? 36
We Are Getting Older? 38
Glossary 40
Index 41

HOW DO WE KNOW
What We Are Made Of?

The ancient Greeks believed that the universe was made of four elements: air, water, fire, and earth. They thought that the human body was made of four corresponding fluids, called humors: blood (air), phlegm (water), yellow bile (fire), and black bile (earth). In the 17th century, helped by the newly-invented microscope, scientists were able to look more closely at body **tissues**. At first, they thought tissues were composed of threadlike fibers, like a piece of material. Later, they saw that tissues were, in fact, formed from millions of tiny units. But they did not know what these were or how they worked. It was not until the 19th century that the true nature of cells, the building blocks and powerhouses of every living thing, began to be understood.

Body ingredients
Every part of your body is made of cells, grouped together to form tissues and **organs**. About 70% of each cell is water.

Dissection
The only way of finding out what a human body is made of is to dissect one. Early doctors were not allowed to dissect human bodies. They based their theories on animal dissections.

Aristotle
The Greek philosopher and scientist, Aristotle (about 384–322 B.C.), formed many theories about the human body that influenced scientific thought for centuries.

Four humors
The ancient Greeks believed the human body was made up of four liquids, called humors: blood, phlegm, yellow bile, and black bile. Good health depended on a good balance of humors.

UNDER THE MICROSCOPE

Cork cells

Robert Hooke
The British physicist Robert Hooke (1635–1703) was the first person to use the word *cell* to describe the tiny units he saw under his microscope. He was studying thin slices of cork at the time.

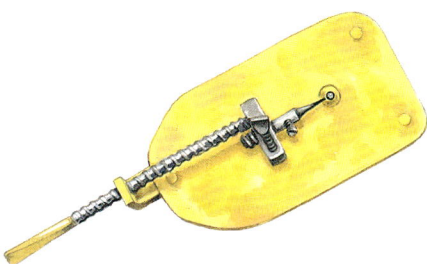

Antoni van Leeuwenhoek
One of the first microscopes was made by a Dutch cloth merchant, Antoni van Leeuwenhoek (1632–1723). He learned how to grind lenses from opticians who made eyeglasses.

Modern microscopes
Van Leeuwenhoek's microscope has a magnification of 200 times. Modern electron microscopes, pioneered in the 1930s, can magnify many thousands of times. They use beams of **electrons** instead of light rays to see things in detail.

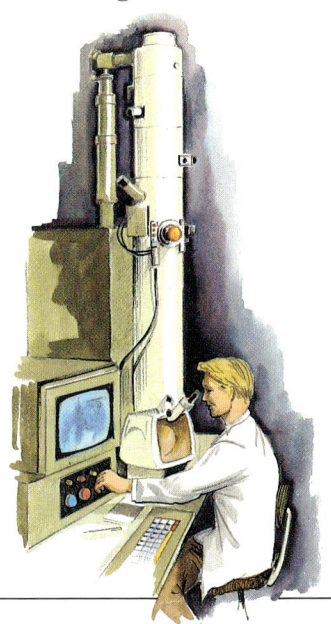

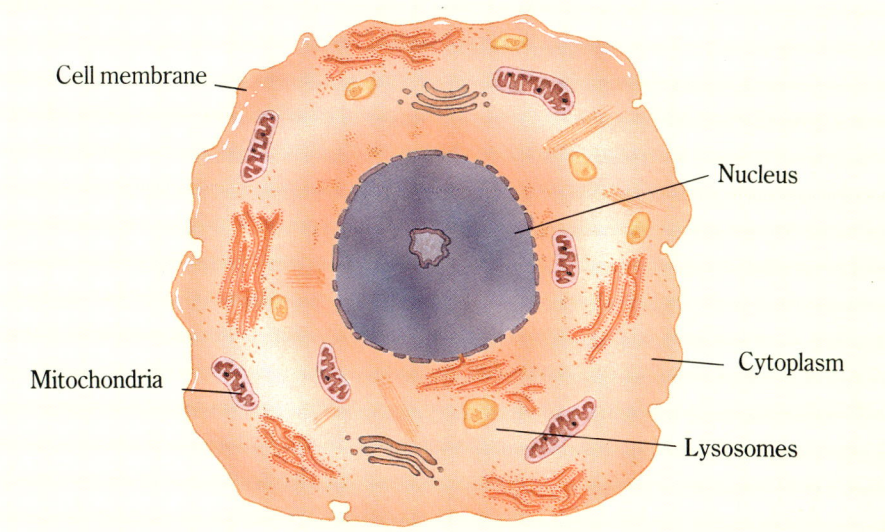

THE VARIETY OF CELLS

The human body consists of about 50 trillion cells. Not only are these the building blocks of the body, but all chemical processes of life take place inside them. The various types of cells share the same basic structure (shown above) but differ in size and shape, depending on their function in the body. The largest cells are female egg cells, or ova, which can just be seen with the naked eye. The smallest cells are in the brain. They measure 0.0002 of an inch (0.005 mm) across.

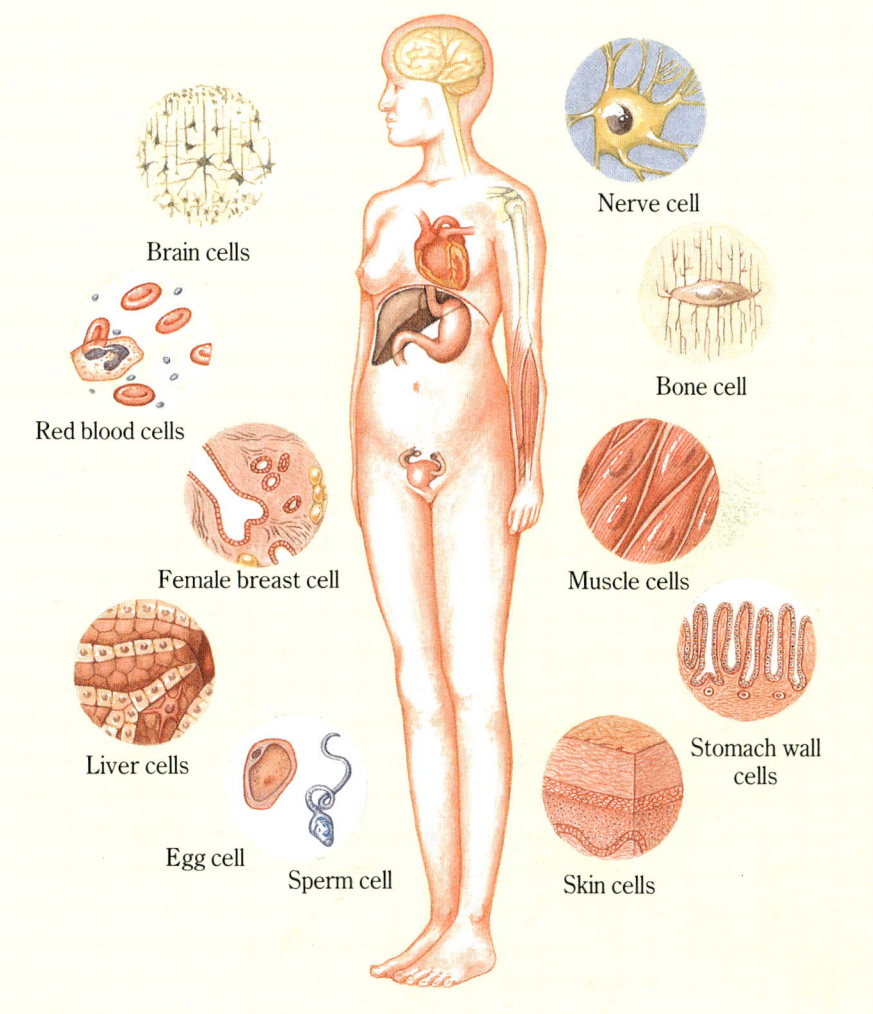

HOW DO WE KNOW
Why We Can Stand Up?

Without a framework to support it, a structure, such as a skyscraper or a bridge, would not be able to stand. The same applies to the human body. Instead of iron or concrete, however, your body's framework consists of bones, which form your skeleton. It holds you up, gives you your distinctive shape, and protects delicate organs, such as your heart, brain, and **spinal cord**. Your skeleton also enables you to move, working in partnership with your muscles.

Animals with backbones and skeletons inside their bodies are known as vertebrates. But most animals (about 90%) are invertebrates. Some, such as beetles, crabs, and snails, have hard cases, called exoskeletons, on the outside of their bodies. These fulfill a similar function to our internal skeletons. Other invertebrates, such as jellyfish, are soft-bodied. On land, their bodies would simply collapse. In the ocean, however, the water provides the support they need.

ANDREAS VESALIUS
The Flemish **anatomist**, Andreas Vesalius (1514–1564), was the first to realize that, in order to treat illness, the structure of the human body had to be understood. In 1543 he published his book, *De Humani Corporis Fabrica (On the Structure of the Human Body)*. In it he described the structure of a human body outward from the foundations of its skeleton, stating that, "as poles are to tents and walls are to houses, so are bones to living creatures."

Anatomy and archaeology
Vesalius's earliest studies were of animal bones and the bones of criminals who had been executed. He later dug up and stole bodies from cemeteries to help him with his studies. Anatomists are not the only scientists interested in bones, however. From fossilized bones and ancient graves, archaeologists have been able to piece together a picture of how the earliest people evolved, how long they lived, what they ate, and how they died.

JOINTS

Joints allow your body to twist, turn, and bend. These are places where two bones meet, such as in your knees, elbows, and fingers. Bones are held in place by strong tissues, called ligaments.

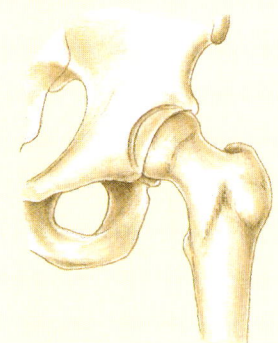

Ball-and-socket
Your shoulders and hips are examples of ball-and-socket joints. They move in all directions.

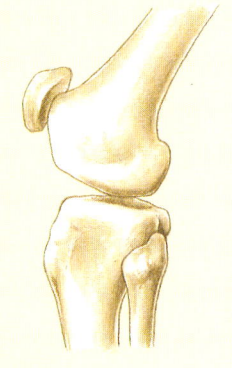

Hinge
Your knees and elbows are hinge joints. Like door hinges, they can only open and shut. Most joints move, but there are some that are immovable, such as those in your skull.

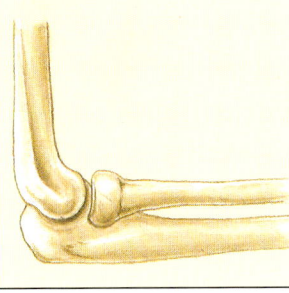

THE SKELETON

An adult's skeleton is made up of 206 separate bones. There are over 300 bones in a newborn baby's skeleton, but some of these later fuse together. For its weight, bone is one of the toughest materials known, stronger than steel or concrete. It is also a living structure, able to knit itself back together if it is broken.

Protective measures
Various parts of your skeleton serve as armor to protect delicate internal organs.

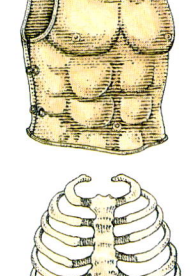

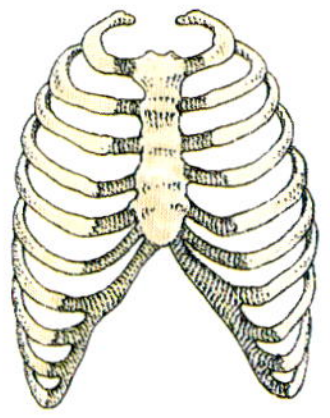

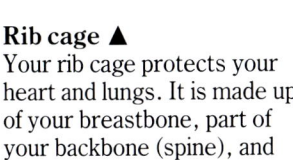

Rib cage ▲
Your rib cage protects your heart and lungs. It is made up of your breastbone, part of your backbone (spine), and 12 pairs of ribs.

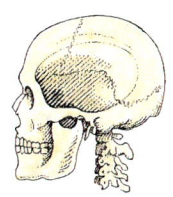

Skull ▲
The cranium, the upper part of your skull, provides strong, helmetlike protection for your brain.

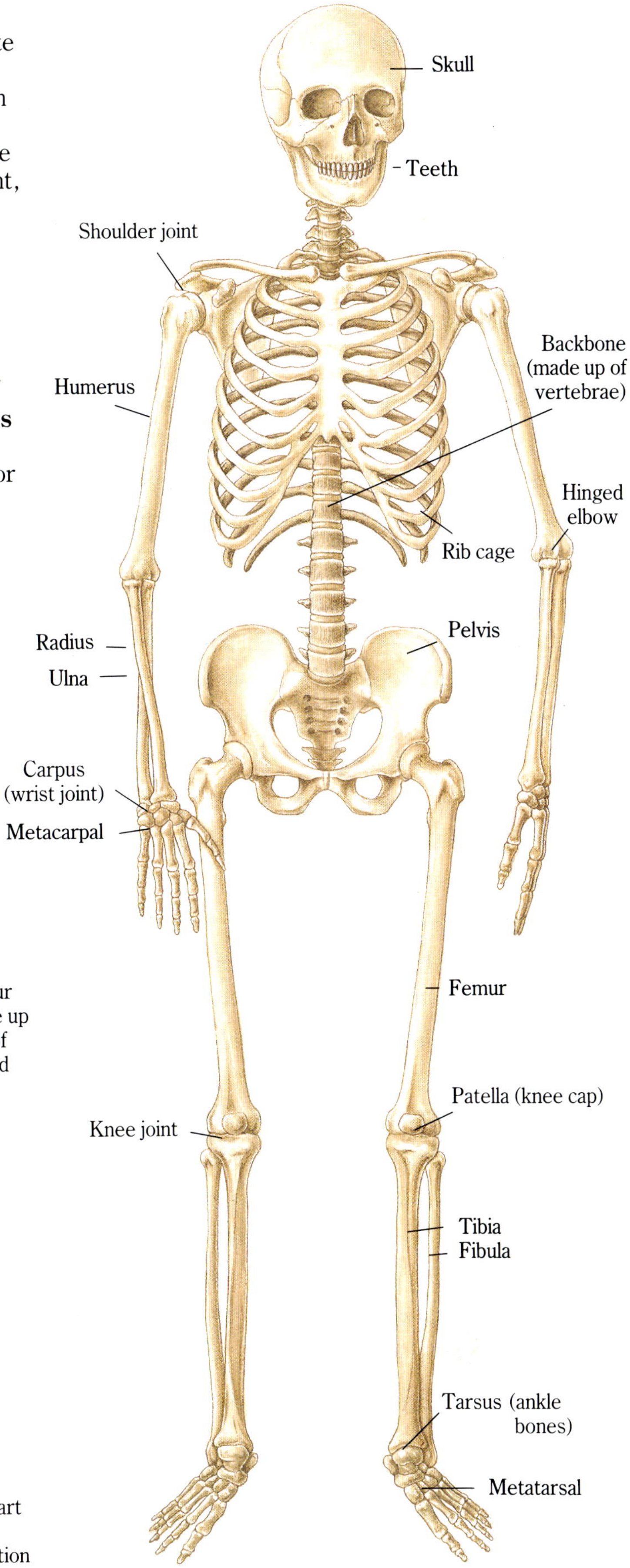

- Skull
- Teeth
- Shoulder joint
- Humerus
- Backbone (made up of vertebrae)
- Hinged elbow
- Rib cage
- Radius
- Ulna
- Pelvis
- Carpus (wrist joint)
- Metacarpal
- Femur
- Patella (knee cap)
- Knee joint
- Tibia
- Fibula
- Tarsus (ankle bones)
- Metatarsal

7

HOW DO WE KNOW
Muscles Help Us Move?

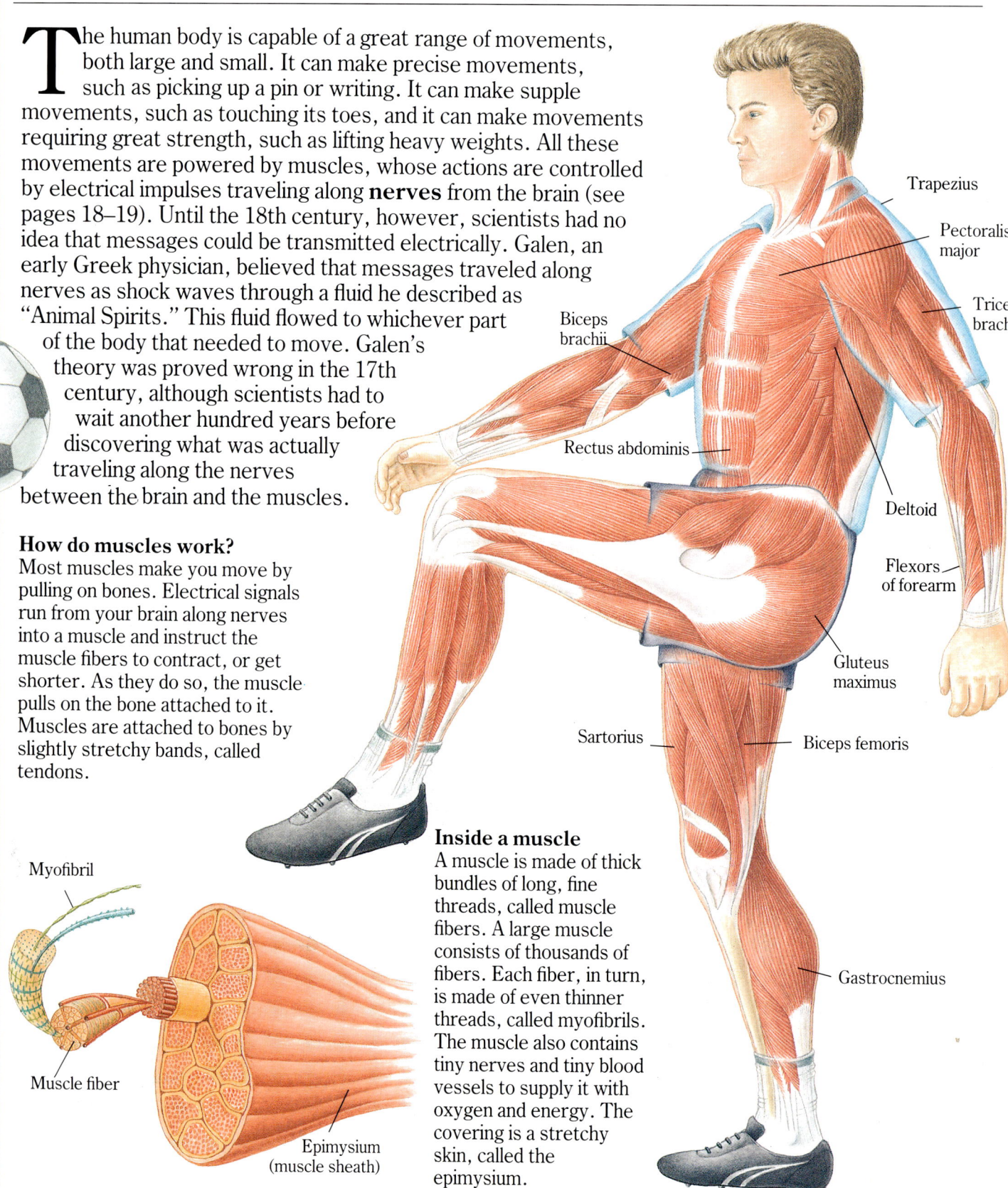

The human body is capable of a great range of movements, both large and small. It can make precise movements, such as picking up a pin or writing. It can make supple movements, such as touching its toes, and it can make movements requiring great strength, such as lifting heavy weights. All these movements are powered by muscles, whose actions are controlled by electrical impulses traveling along **nerves** from the brain (see pages 18–19). Until the 18th century, however, scientists had no idea that messages could be transmitted electrically. Galen, an early Greek physician, believed that messages traveled along nerves as shock waves through a fluid he described as "Animal Spirits." This fluid flowed to whichever part of the body that needed to move. Galen's theory was proved wrong in the 17th century, although scientists had to wait another hundred years before discovering what was actually traveling along the nerves between the brain and the muscles.

How do muscles work?
Most muscles make you move by pulling on bones. Electrical signals run from your brain along nerves into a muscle and instruct the muscle fibers to contract, or get shorter. As they do so, the muscle pulls on the bone attached to it. Muscles are attached to bones by slightly stretchy bands, called tendons.

Inside a muscle
A muscle is made of thick bundles of long, fine threads, called muscle fibers. A large muscle consists of thousands of fibers. Each fiber, in turn, is made of even thinner threads, called myofibrils. The muscle also contains tiny nerves and tiny blood vessels to supply it with oxygen and energy. The covering is a stretchy skin, called the epimysium.

Pulling in pairs

Muscles can only pull on bones. They cannot push them back again. This is why many muscles work in pairs. To bend your arm, for example, your biceps muscle contracts and pulls. Meanwhile, its partner, the triceps, relaxes to allow your arm to move. To straighten your arm again, your biceps relaxes and your triceps contracts.

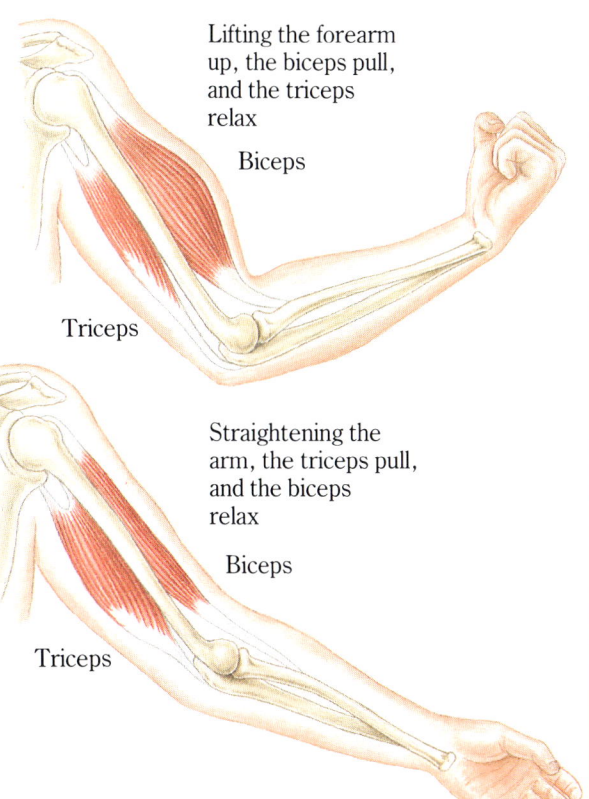

Lifting the forearm up, the biceps pull, and the triceps relax

Biceps

Triceps

Straightening the arm, the triceps pull, and the biceps relax

Biceps

Triceps

PULLING FACES

The 30 or so muscles in your face do not pull on bones. They pull on your skin to change your expression. They help you to frown, smile, and raise your eyebrows.

You use more muscles in your face when you frown than when you smile.

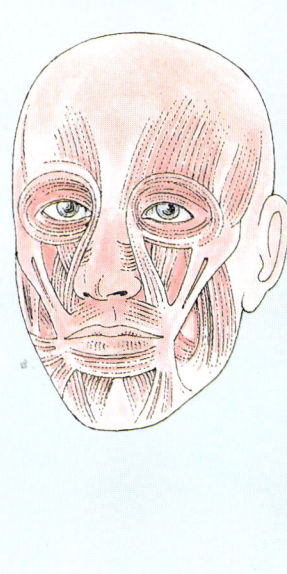

Types of muscles

There are more than 600 muscles in your body. Some lie just under your skin. They pull on muscles to make you move. Others are found deep inside your body. They help you to breathe, digest your food, control your bladder, and so on. Muscles that you control, such as those that move your arms and legs, are called voluntary muscles. Those that work automatically, such as the heart, are called involuntary muscles.

Skeletal

Skeletal muscles are muscles that pull on your bones to move the various parts of your body. This muscle is known as striped muscle because it looks striped under a microscope.

Heart

The muscle in your heart is called cardiac muscle. Unlike the muscles in your arms and legs, it never tires but keeps your heart beating constantly and regularly.

Smooth

Muscles that control internal organs, such as your bladder, are made of smooth muscle.

Schwammerdamm's nerve

In the 17th century, the Dutch scientist Jan Schwammerdamm (1637–1685) made an important discovery. By stimulating the cut end of a nerve, he made a muscle contract. However, he had no idea that the movement was caused by electrical signals. He thought it was simply a mechanical reaction.

Galvani's frogs

In the 18th century, an Italian professor of anatomy, Luigi Galvani (1737–1798), found that the muscles in a frog's legs could be made to move when a spark of electricity was applied. The link between electricity and muscle movement had been found.

Luigi Galvani

When the frog's legs were touched with a metal scalpel that had been in contact with a static electricity machine, they jerked violently.

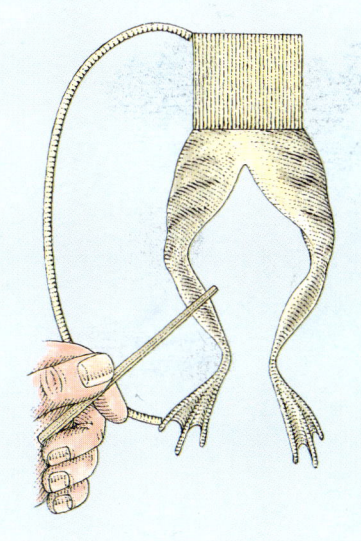

HOW DO WE KNOW
What Flows in Our Veins?

If you cut yourself, a slightly sticky, reddish liquid called blood oozes out. Don't worry, you can afford to lose a little blood. After all, you have about 5.5 quarts (5 l) of it flowing throughout your body. Blood is your body's transportation network. It carries the gas oxygen from your lungs to your cells and waste carbon dioxide gas back to your lungs. It carries water, **nutrients**, and hormones (see pages 36–37), around your body. White blood cells help to fight infection.

The ancient Greeks believed blood to be the most important of the four humors. In the 17th century, van Leeuwenhoek observed red blood cells under his microscope. But scientists still thought that blood was a pure liquid. We now know that red, and many white, blood cells are made in the bone marrow. About 3 million new red blood cells are produced every second.

Blood transfusions
The first blood **transfusions** were carried out in the 17th century. A French court **physician** transfused blood from a lamb into a human patient, who later died. Transfusions were then banned by the church for being too risky. The first successful blood transfusion took place in 1825. Blood was syringed from one person to another.

Blood Groups
Early blood transfusions were hit-and-miss, because no one realized that there were different types of blood. Unless a matching blood type is received, the results of a transfusion can be fatal. The first person to realize this was an Austrian scientist, Karl Landsteiner, in the 1920s. There are now 14 different systems of classifying blood. One system divides blood into four main groups: A, B, O, and AB.

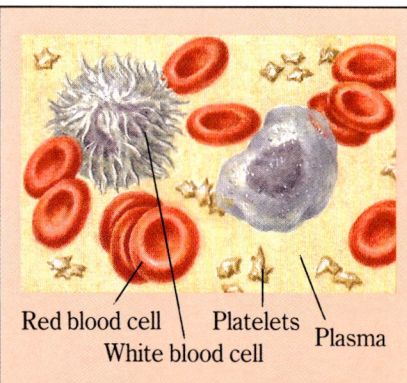

Red blood cell | Platelets
White blood cell | Plasma

WHAT'S IN BLOOD
Blood is composed of a mixture of cells, floating in a yellowish liquid called plasma. Plasma is mostly water, with nutrients and salts dissolved in it. It makes up about half of your blood. The rest consists of red and white blood cells and platelets. Red blood cells carry oxygen through your body. White blood cells' main purpose is to fight infection (see page 31). Platelets are fragments of cells that help blood to clot.

LEECHES AND BLOODLETTING
In the 18th and 19th centuries, bloodletting was the most popular treatment for fevers and other types of illnesses. Leeches were used to suck patients' blood. The leeches' saliva contains a chemical that stops blood from clotting so that it flows freely.

A medicinal leech (*Hirudo medicinalis*)

Blood vessels

Blood flows through your body in a vast network of tubes, called blood vessels. There are about 58,000 miles (96,000 km) of blood vessels in your body. There are different types of blood vessels, including arteries, veins, and capillaries. Oxygen-rich blood flows from your heart through arteries. Blood containing carbon dioxide flows back to your heart in your veins. The arteries branch into finer tubes, called capillaries. Their walls are so thin that oxygen can easily pass through them from your blood into your cells. The capillaries join up again to form veins.

Capillary discovery

Until the 4th century, scientists thought arteries and veins were the same thing. They had no knowledge of capillaries at all. This discovery had to wait until 1661, when Marcello Malpighi saw the capillaries in a frog's lung under his microscope.

A Pulse Rate

You can feel that your blood is circulated around your body. Use your fingertips to find a beat in your wrist, just like a doctor does. This beat proves that your blood is being pumped around your body through all the blood vessels. You can tell how often your heart beats per minute by counting the pulses.

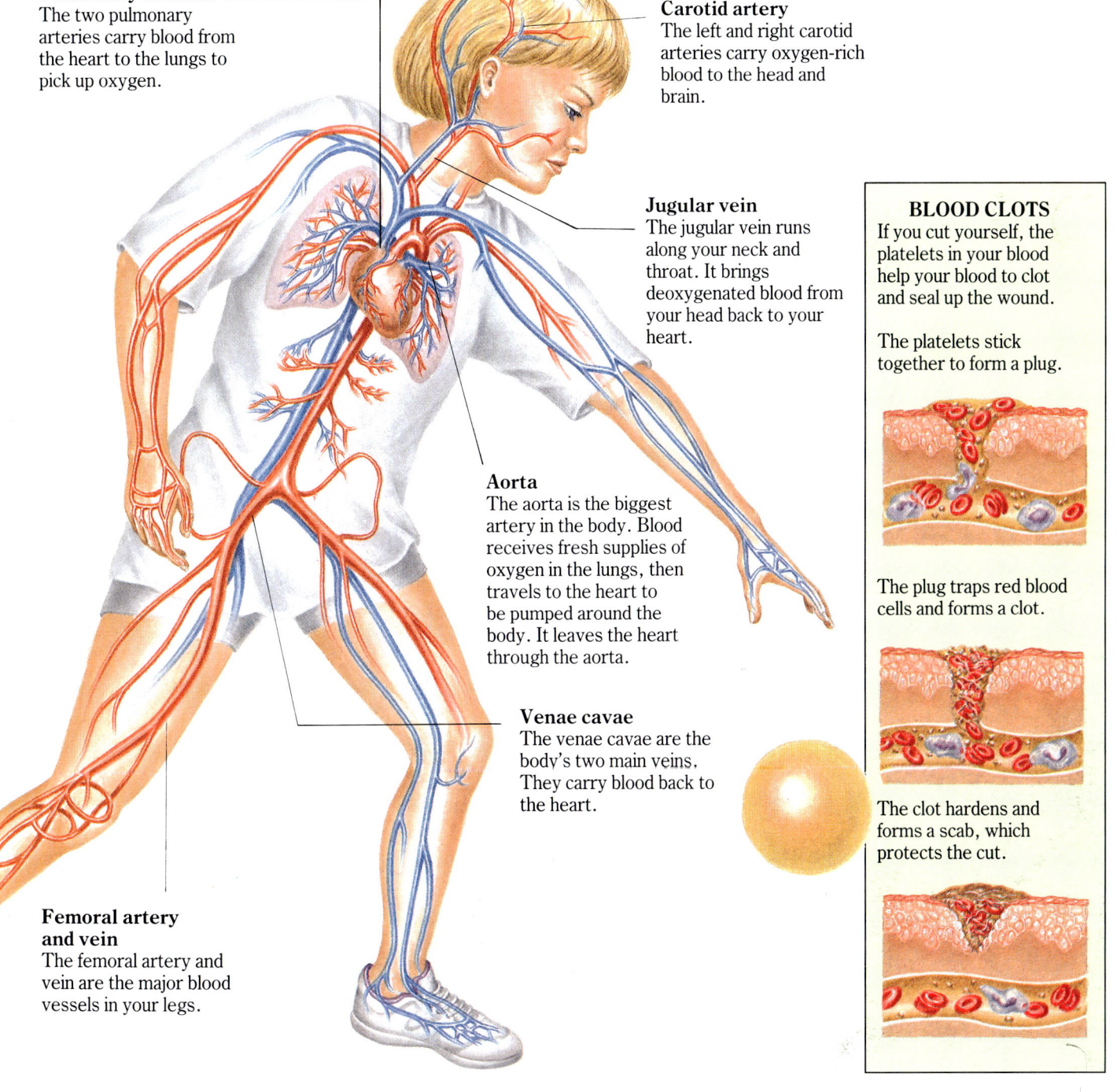

Pulmonary arteries
The two pulmonary arteries carry blood from the heart to the lungs to pick up oxygen.

Carotid artery
The left and right carotid arteries carry oxygen-rich blood to the head and brain.

Jugular vein
The jugular vein runs along your neck and throat. It brings deoxygenated blood from your head back to your heart.

Aorta
The aorta is the biggest artery in the body. Blood receives fresh supplies of oxygen in the lungs, then travels to the heart to be pumped around the body. It leaves the heart through the aorta.

Venae cavae
The venae cavae are the body's two main veins. They carry blood back to the heart.

Femoral artery and vein
The femoral artery and vein are the major blood vessels in your legs.

BLOOD CLOTS

If you cut yourself, the platelets in your blood help your blood to clot and seal up the wound.

The platelets stick together to form a plug.

The plug traps red blood cells and forms a clot.

The clot hardens and forms a scab, which protects the cut.

HOW DO WE KNOW
Blood Moves Through the Body?

For Galen in the 2nd century A.D., the heart was a furnace where air and blood met and created heat. This warmed the blood and gave it energy. It was not until the 1620s that an English doctor, William Harvey, discovered the true function of the heart as a muscular pump that pushes blood throughout the body.

Harvey was also the first person to realize that blood flows through the body in a continuous circle, not along two separate paths as had previously been believed. At the time, people thought Harvey was crazy. But his discovery was one of the most important and far-reaching ever made in medical science.

We now know that Harvey was right and that the heart pumps blood through complex systems of arteries and veins. Arteries branch out into arterioles, and veins branch into tiny venules.

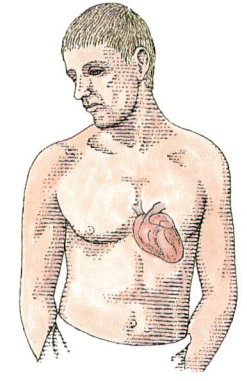

Seat of the soul
For centuries, people believed that the heart was the seat of the soul and the body's center of wisdom and intelligence. The brain was simply seen as an organ for cooling the heart down so that it could work properly.

William Harvey
William Harvey (1578–1657) was the first person to prove the **circulation** of the blood and the heart's role as a pump. He published his findings in a book called *Anatomica de Motu Cordis et Sanguinis (The Movement of the Heart and Blood)*. People were appalled by his theories, and his medical practice suffered as a result. However, Harvey became a royal physician and was able to continue his studies.

Pumps and machines
William Harvey (left) may have been influenced in his discovery of the heart as a pump by the pumping machines (right) used in mining, engineering, and fire fighting in the 17th century. Such machines had not even been invented in Galen's time.

VALVES AND VEINS
Galen believed that blood could flow backward and forward in the veins. Harvey realized that tiny **valves** inside the veins made this impossible.

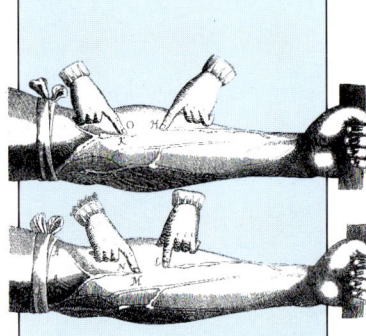

He proved this by tying a **tourniquet** around his arm. It was tight enough to stop blood from flowing out from the arm through the veins but still allowed blood to flow into the arm through the arteries. The veins below the tourniquet swelled with blood. The veins above the tourniquet stayed empty.

Inside the heart

Your heart is divided into two halves. The left side pumps oxygen-rich blood from your lungs throughout your body. The right side receives blood from your body and pumps it to your lungs to be replenished with oxygen. Each half is divided into two chambers: an atrium and a ventricle. Galen thought that blood passed from the right to the left side of the heart through tiny holes in the dividing wall. Harvey realized there was too much blood for this to happen, and that a circulatory system must be involved. Harvey also worked out that the heart fills up and empties with blood by muscular contraction. The theory at the time was that the heart worked like a syringe, filling up with blood drawn from the liver.

Have a heart
Your heart is in the middle of your chest, slightly to the left of center. It is about the size of a clenched fist.

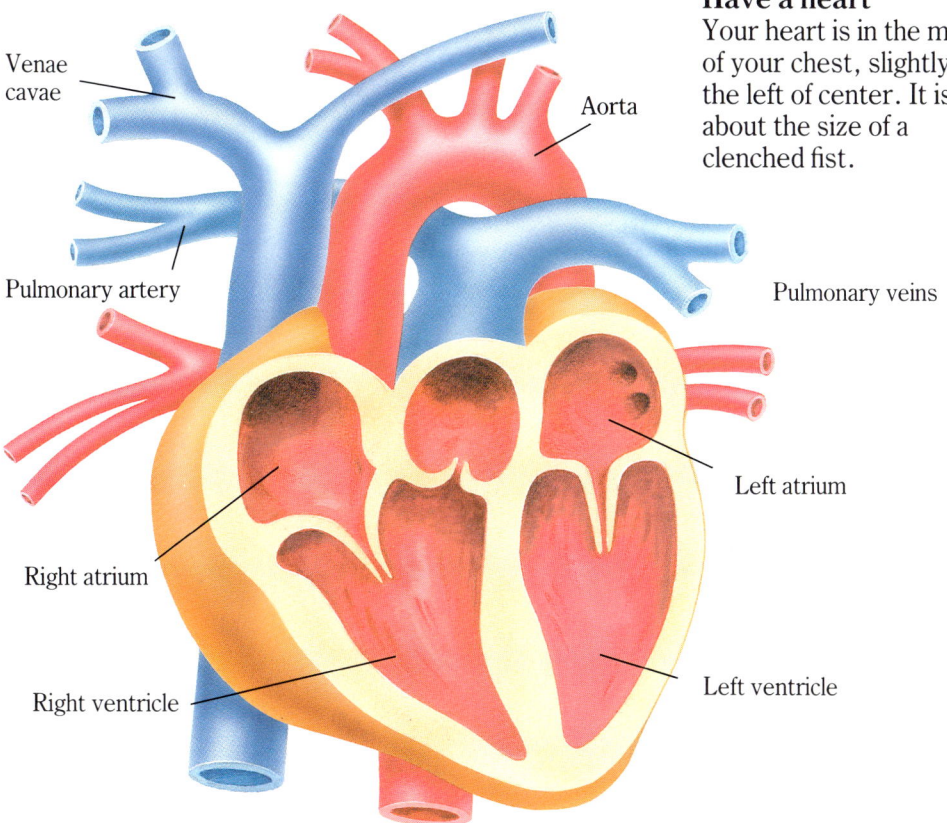

Venae cavae
Aorta
Pulmonary artery
Pulmonary veins
Left atrium
Right atrium
Right ventricle
Left ventricle

One-way flow
Valves are small flaps on the inside walls of your heart and some blood vessels. They allow blood to flow in only one direction.

The flow of blood pushes the valve open so it can pass through.

When the blood has flowed through the valve, the flaps snap shut to stop a backward flow.

No control
You cannot control the muscles in your heart. That is, you can't make them stop beating. The muscle in the heart is very specialized. It is called a voluntary muscle because it keeps working without you having to think about it.

THE STETHOSCOPE
Today doctors use stethoscopes to listen to your heart and lungs in order to make sure that they are working properly. The first stethoscope was invented in 1816 by a French doctor, René Laënnec. He experimented first with a tube made of rolled-up sheets of writing paper, then with a wooden tube.

The modern two-ear stethoscope (below) was devised in the United States in 1850. Like its predecessor, it works by amplifying the sounds made by the heart and lungs.

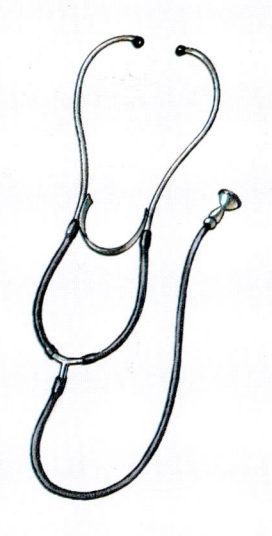

HOW DO WE KNOW
There's Air in Our Lungs?

You breathe all the time, drawing fresh air into your lungs and pushing stale air out. If you tried to hold your breath for longer than a few minutes, your brain would override you and make you start breathing again. Early doctors and scientists realized that air (one of the four humors of the ancient Greeks) was vital to the human body. But they thought that the function of air was to cool the fire inside the heart to prevent it from going out. This was the fire that Galen believed "cooked" food and turned it into blood. We know now that the oxygen in air is used by the cells for respiration. This is the process by which the cells use oxygen to release energy from food. During respiration, a waste gas, carbon dioxide, is produced. This gas is removed from your body when you breathe out. Oxygen, food, and carbon dioxide travel through your body in your blood.

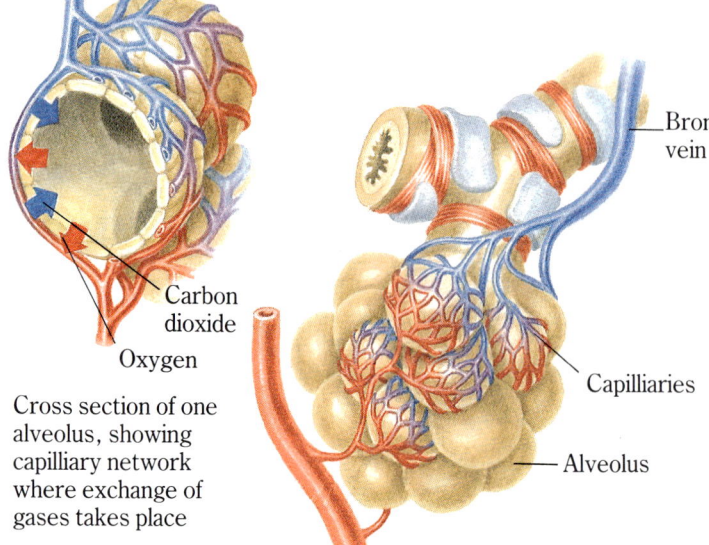

Cross section of one alveolus, showing capilliary network where exchange of gases takes place

The bronchiole and alveoli found at the end of the bronchi

Respiratory system
When you breathe in, air goes through your nose or mouth and down your trachea (windpipe). Then it travels through two tubes (bronchi) into your two lungs. These parts make up your respiratory system.

When you breathe normally, you only use about one-sixth of your lung capacity.

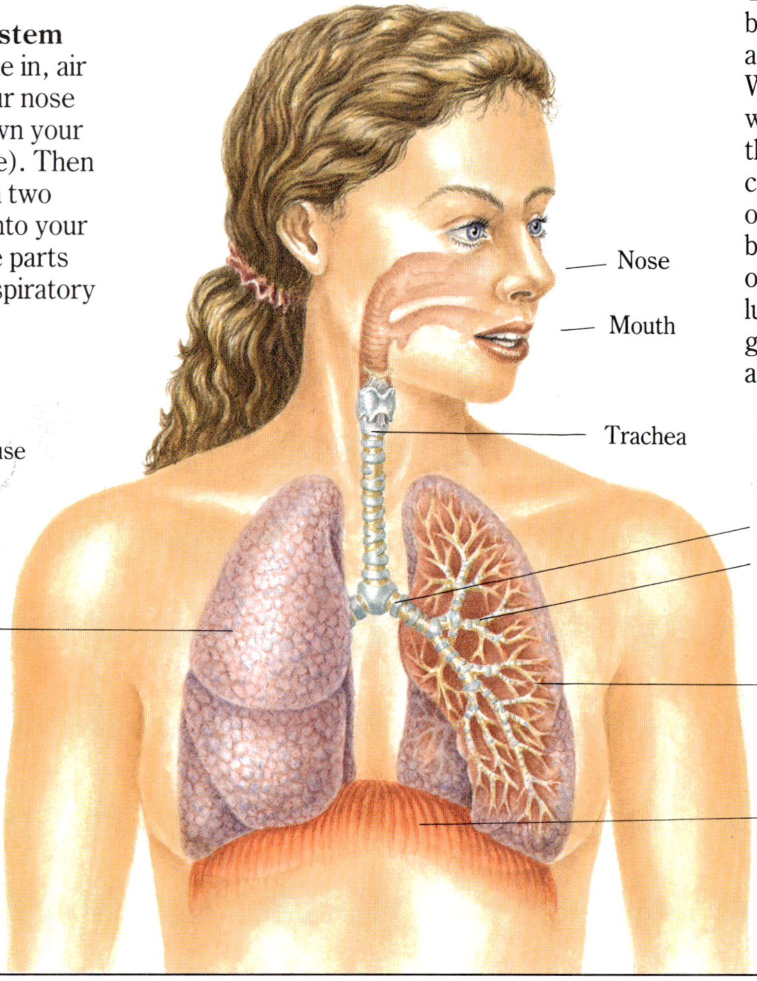

Amazing alveoli
The bronchi divide into many tiny, branching tubes. Each tube ends in a bunch of air sacs, called alveoli. When you breathe in, the alveoli fill with air. Oxygen from the air passes through their walls and into the capillaries surrounding them. The oxygen is then carried through the body. Carbon dioxide passes the other way to be breathed out. Each lung has about 300 million alveoli, giving it a huge surface area for absorbing oxygen.

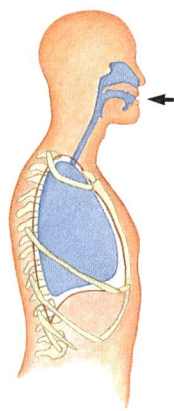

Breathing in (inhaling)
When you breathe in, your diaphragm (the sheet of muscle under your chest) contracts and moves down. At the same time, your ribs move up and out. Air is sucked into the increased space in your chest.

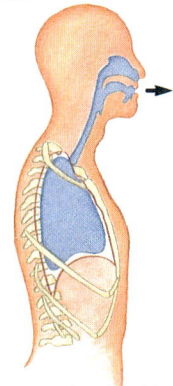

Breathing out (exhaling)
When you breathe out, your diaphragm expands and moves up. Your ribs move down and inward to decrease the space in your chest. This action pushes the stale air out of your lungs.

How much air?
Your lungs can hold about 3 quarts (3 l) of air, but you only breathe about half a quart (0.5 l) of air in or out at a time. When you exercise, this amount increases dramatically to provide your muscles with the extra energy they need.

3-quart containers

BREATHING—FACT AND FICTION

Galen
Galen was born in about A.D. 130 in Greece but worked in Rome, where he was, among other things, a surgeon to the gladiators. Many of his theories were accepted for centuries. Galen realized the importance of air to the body but had no knowledge of oxygen or respiration.

Hooke's experiment
Robert Hooke conducted a series of experiments to show how chest movements were responsible for filling the lungs with air. He cut open a dog's chest so that its ribs could not move. Air had to be pumped artificially into the dog's lungs to keep it alive.

Joseph Priestley
Joseph Priestley (1733–1804), an English **chemist**, was the first person to discover the gas oxygen in 1774. The discovery was made simultaneously by a Swedish chemist, Karl Scheele. Oxygen makes up about 21% of the air we breathe in.

Lavoisier's breakthrough
A French chemist, Antoine Lavoisier (1743–1794), took Priestley's discovery a step further in 1787. He was able to prove that, just as fire needs oxygen to burn, so respiration depends on oxygen to release energy from food. Despite his momentous discovery, Lavoisier met an unusual end. He was guillotined in 1794, during the French Revolution.

HOW DO WE KNOW
Why We Have to Eat?

Food is the fuel your body needs to keep it running smoothly, just as a car needs gasoline. Without the energy supplied by regular supplies of food, your body would slow down and eventually grind to a halt. Food also contains nutrients that your body needs for growth, repair, and good health. Feeling hungry is your brain's way of telling your body that its stores of energy and nutrients are running low.

For energy and nutrients to reach your cells, food has to be broken down into particles small enough to be absorbed into your bloodstream. On page 17, you can see how we now understand the body's digestive system works. Galen's theory of digestion was quite different, however. He believed that food passed from the stomach into the liver, where it was "cooked" and mixed with a substance called "Natural Spirits" to form blood. The blood flowed through the body, distributing the natural spirits, then returned to the liver for fresh supplies.

Malnutrition
Pictures of severely malnourished famine victims in Africa are striking evidence of what happens if people do not have enough to eat. About 15% of the world's population suffer from malnutrition.

A balanced diet
The ancient Greeks believed that a healthy body depended on a balance of the four humors (see page 4). Modern **nutritionists** believe that a balanced diet, containing a combination of foods and nutrients, is what keeps us fit and healthy. The major food groups and their nutritional properties are shown.

Fit to run
Many athletes follow high protein, low fat diets designed to build up their muscles and supply them with plenty of energy. The energy in food is measured in calories. An excess of calories caused by eating too much can make you fat and be harmful to your health.

Vegetables and fruit

Vitamins to prevent disease and keep your body parts healthy

Minerals for healthy teeth, bones, and blood, and for regulating the body's chemical processes

Fats for energy and insulation

Cheese

Eggs

Grains, cereals, peas, and beans

Fiber for a healthy digestive system

Carbohydrates for energy

Nuts

Fish and chicken

Protein for growth and repair

The digestive system

The human digestive system consists of a series of tubes about 30 feet (9 m) long. As food travels through this system, it is broken down into smaller and smaller particles. The digestive process begins as soon as you take a bite of food. It ends with waste material being excreted from your anus. When you swallow, food travels down your esophagus into your stomach, where it stays for three to four hours before passing into your small intestine. Nutrients are absorbed into your blood through the walls of the small intestine. Any undigested food continues its journey through your large intestine to your rectum. An average-sized meal takes about three days to travel through your system.

Mouth
In your mouth, your teeth chop and chew your food. The food is also mixed with saliva, which makes it easier to swallow, and helps break the food down.

Esophagus
As you swallow, food is pushed down your esophagus. A flap of skin, called the epiglottis, covers your trachea (windpipe) to keep food from going down "the wrong way" and making you choke.

Large intestine
Any undigested food passes into your large intestine. Solid waste is stored in your rectum as feces. It is excreted when you go to the bathroom.

Small intestine
The small intestine is narrow but about 13 feet (4 m) long. In the first part of the small intestine (the duodenum), digestive juices act on your food. In the second part of the tube (the ilium), the food passes through the intestine walls and into your bloodstream.

Liver
Your liver makes bile, a green liquid that breaks down fats as they pass through your small intestine. Blood full of freshly-digested food passes into your liver before it goes to the rest of your body. Your body sorts the nutrients out and stores some for later use.

Pancreas
Your pancreas makes digestive juices that act on the food in your duodenum.

Stomach
Food travels down your esophagus into your stomach, a stretchy, muscular pouch. Here it is mixed with **enzymes** and acids to break it down further. This process leaves the contents of your stomach looking like thick, creamy soup.

VITAL VITAMINS
In 1897, a Dutch doctor, Christiaan Eijkmann, discovered the group of vitamins known as vitamin B. He found that a lack of vitamin B in food caused the disease beri-beri. This was the first time doctors suspected that food, as well as germs, could be responsible for illness. Eijkmann was awarded the Nobel Prize for his work.

Vitamin supplements
About 20 vitamins have been discovered so far. People on diets, or who are not eating properly because of illness, often take vitamin pills to make sure they are getting enough.

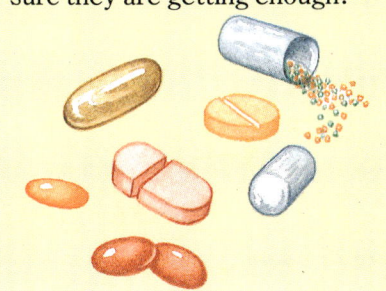

17

HOW DO WE KNOW
What Controls Our Body?

Every move you make and everything you do, think, feel, and remember is controlled by your brain. This amazing organ can receive, store, and process more information than the most powerful computer. Messages, in the form of electrical signals, speed back and forth between your body and your brain along a network of millions of nerve cells. It's no wonder that, despite making up only 2% of your body weight, your brain uses up a fifth of your energy! Scientists who study the brain are called neurologists. Since the end of the 19th century, many of the brain's secrets have been discovered. But large areas are still a mystery.

The brain
The human brain weighs about 3.3 pounds (1.5 kg) whether you are a genius or not! It looks like a lump of grayish jelly covered with deep grooves and wrinkles. Until 1861, scientists thought that the brain acted as a whole to control the body. Then a French anatomist, Paul Broca, discovered that different parts of the brain had different jobs to do.

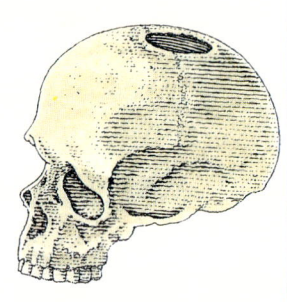

BRAIN SURGERY IN HISTORY
The earliest form of brain surgery involved cutting a hole in a person's skull to release the "evil spirits" believed to cause illnesses. This process is called trepanning. The earliest trepanned skull found dates from about 5000 B.C.

Heart or brain?
Aristotle, in common with many ancient scientists, believed the heart to be the body's control center. This theory was only challenged in the 1620s, when Harvey discovered the heart's function as a pump. Even then, doctors had no real idea of the brain's role in the body.

Cerebral cortex
Divided into two halves, called hemispheres, the cerebral cortex controls movement, the senses, intelligence, and emotions.

Thalamus
The thalamus is the part of your brain that senses and responds to pain.

Cerebellum
The cerebellum controls movement and coordination.

Hypothalamus
This keeps your body temperature constant and deals with feelings of hunger and thirst. It also controls the release of **hormones** from the pituitary gland.

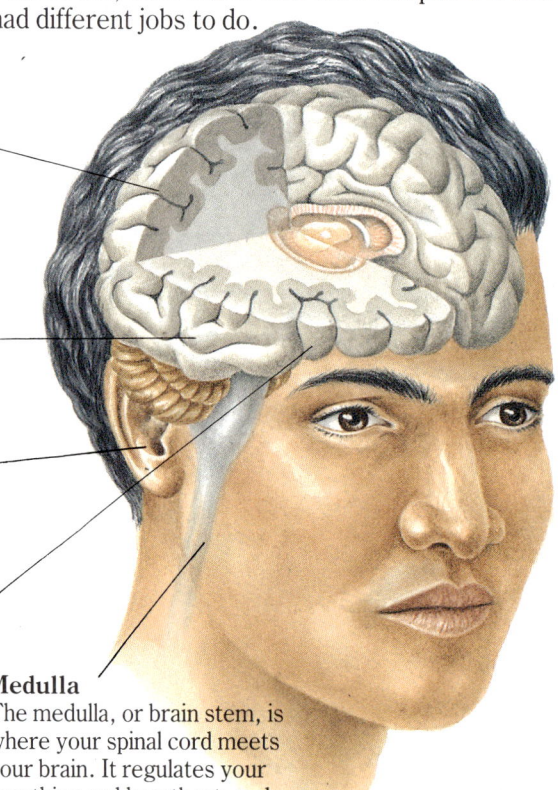

Medulla
The medulla, or brain **stem**, is where your spinal cord **meets** your brain. It regulates **your** breathing and heartbeat, and controls reflex actions, such as sneezing and coughing.

Brain centers
The brain is divided into areas, called centers. Each center does a different job. Motor centers send messages to your muscles. Sensory centers process messages from your sense organs.

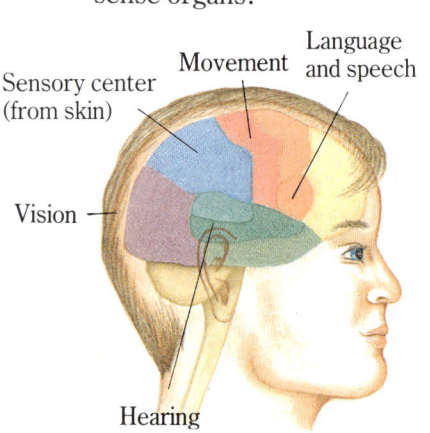

18

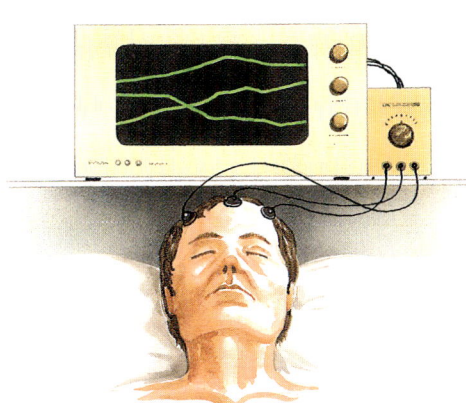

Brain scans
The brain's electrical activity can be traced using a machine, called an electroencephalograph (EEG). **Electrodes** are attached to a patient's head and the electrical impulses recorded and traced on a screen. Any irregularities in the pattern of impulses can be detected. The EEG machine was invented in 1929.

Lumps and bumps
In the late 18th century, an Austrian doctor, Franz Joseph Gall, founded the practice of phrenology. Gall believed that you could tell a lot about people's characters and abilities by feeling and measuring the bony bumps of their skulls. He divided the skull into 37 areas. Each area represented a certain characteristic.

THE NERVOUS SYSTEM
Your brain sends out and receives messages through your nerves and spinal cord. This is your nervous system. Its function was first understood by two Greek doctors, Erasistratus and Herophilus, in the 4th century B.C.

Brain
Your brain controls your entire nervous system. Together with your spinal cord, it is known as your **central nervous system**.

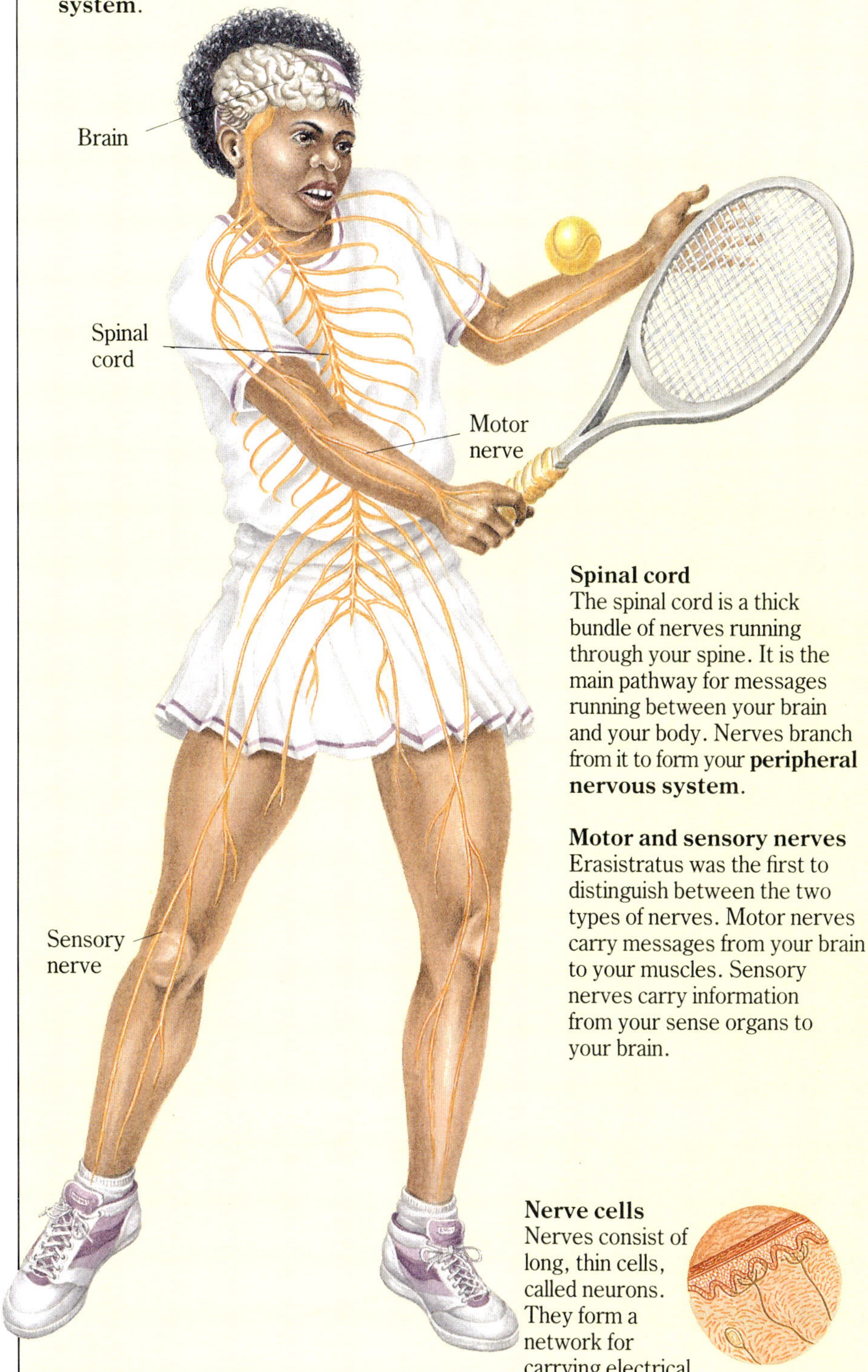

Spinal cord
The spinal cord is a thick bundle of nerves running through your spine. It is the main pathway for messages running between your brain and your body. Nerves branch from it to form your **peripheral nervous system**.

Motor and sensory nerves
Erasistratus was the first to distinguish between the two types of nerves. Motor nerves carry messages from your brain to your muscles. Sensory nerves carry information from your sense organs to your brain.

Nerve cells
Nerves consist of long, thin cells, called neurons. They form a network for carrying electrical signals throughout your body.

HOW DO WE KNOW
What We Feel?

Your sense of touch is spread all over your body in your skin. You soon know about it if you touch something very hot or very cold. But you can also feel textures, such as smooth, rough, or slimy, and pressure, from a light brush against something to a heavy weight pressing down on you. You can also feel pain, which serves to warn you that possible injury is being done to your body. All these sensations are detected by **sensory receptors** in your skin. The messages are passed along your nerves to your brain for processing. Your brain can then inform you, through your nerves and muscles, if you need to take action. This might mean letting go of a hot object before it burns you.

DENTISTS' DISCOVERY

Two American dentists were among the first people to use **anesthetics** to numb the pain of surgery. In 1844, Horace Wells (1815–1848) used laughing gas (nitrous oxide) to pull teeth painlessly. In 1846, his pupil, William Morton (1819–1868), invented the first anesthetic machine, using sponges soaked in the chemical ether.

Horace Wells

The story of anesthetics

There is a tiny gap, called a synapse, between one nerve and another. Electrical signals have to cross the gap in the form of chemicals, called neurotransmitters. Once across, they change back into electrical signals. This is how pain and other sensations are transmitted. Anesthetics work by preventing messages from crossing synapses so that no pain is felt. Before the pioneering work of Wells and Morton, patients had to be strapped down during operations or given wine or poppy juice to numb the pain. In 1847, a woman was given the anesthetic chloroform to lessen the pain of childbirth. She was so pleased with the result, she named her child Anesthesia.

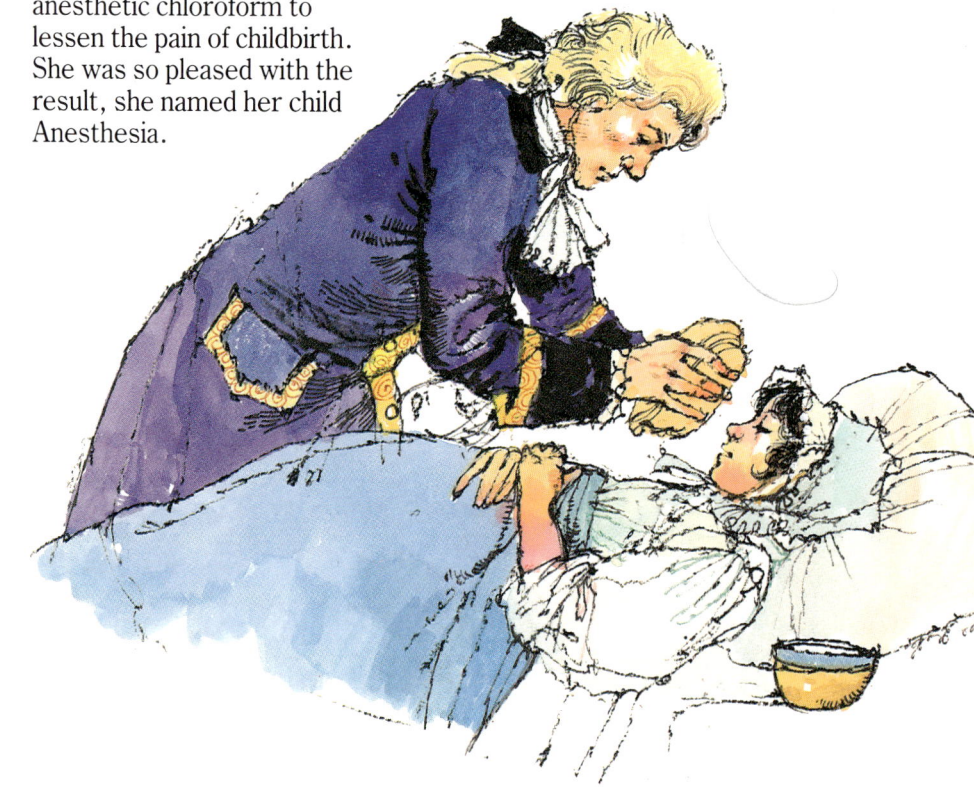

Sensors under your skin

There are millions of nerve sensors under the surface of your skin, each capable of detecting a different type of sensation. Sensors called Meissner's corpuscles respond to light touch. Pacinian corpuscles respond to heavy pressure. Pain is detected by free nerve endings. Sensors called Krause's bulbs and Ruffini's organs respond to temperature. The sensors are not evenly distributed, however, so some parts of your body are much more sensitive than others. The most sensitive areas are your lips, toes, and fingertips. The skin on your back and bottom is the least sensitive on your body.

Reflex actions

If you touch something prickly, like a pin or thistle, you automatically jerk your hand away. This is known as a reflex action. It is a split-second response to protect you from harm. In a reflex action, your nerves bypass your brain and send their messages directly to your muscles, instructing them to act.

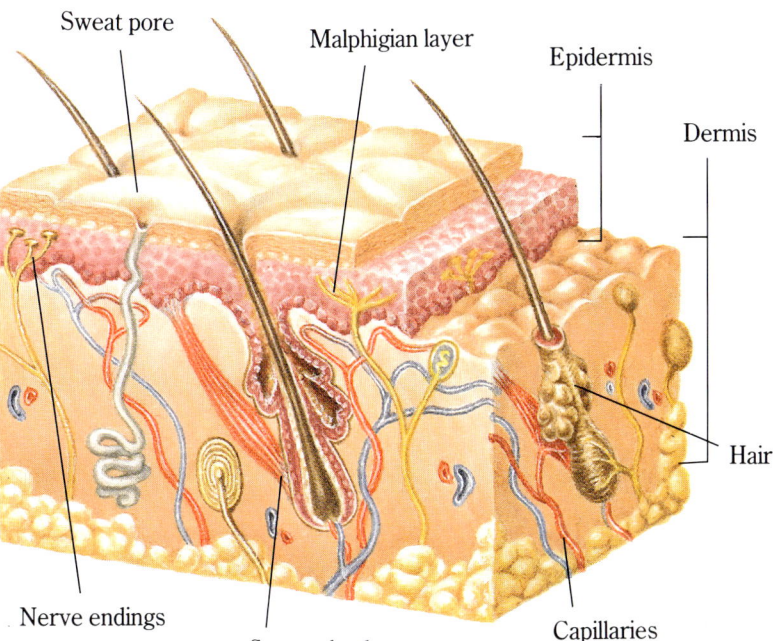

Nerves to the brain

Your nerves carry information from your skin to the sensory center in your brain (see page 19). It is divided into different areas, each dealing with separate messages from different parts of your body.

Other Nerves

Not all nerves have to do with movement and the senses. There is a system of nerves called automatic nerves, which control the many movements of the body that are essential for survival. These nerves make the lungs breathe, the heart pump, control digestion and keep the body temperature even.

Fingertip touch

When you stroke a cat, the sensors in the skin on your fingertips detect the warmth and silkiness of the cat's fur. This information moves along your nerves in your arm, through your spinal cord, and into your brain.

HOW DO WE KNOW
We See What We See?

Aristotle was the first person to make a formal list of the five senses as sight, touch, hearing, smell, and taste. Of the five, our eyesight provides us with most of the information we use to build up a picture of our surroundings. So important are our eyes that things we have seen account for about three-quarters of all the knowledge entering our brains. And yet scientists are only just beginning to understand exactly how the eyes and brain work together to make us see.

Moving eyes
Your eyes are constantly moving, even when they appear to be quite still. Six muscles around each eye coordinate eye movement, so you do not look in two directions at once. Scientists have monitored eye movement by fitting people with mirrored contact lenses and recording the reflections on film. Two types of movement have been seen: involuntary flicks and drifts of the eye and voluntary movements, such as those you make when you are reading this page.

Sclera and cornea
The sclera is the outermost layer of the wall of the eyeball. In front of the eye it covers the cornea, a clear layer that allows light into the eye.

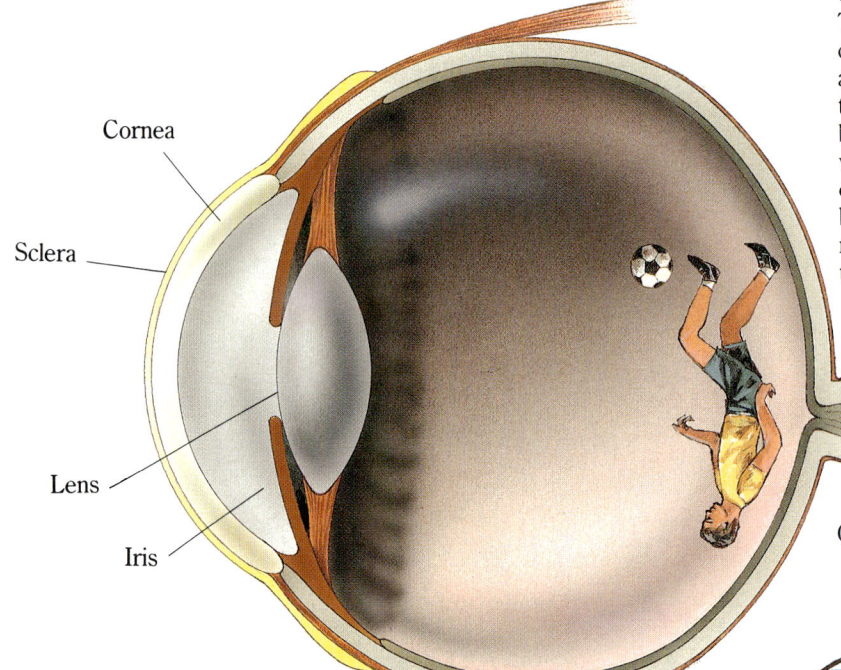

Optic nerve
The optic nerve carries information about the image on the retina to your brain. The point at which it leaves your eye is called your blind spot. There are no rods or cones in this spot.

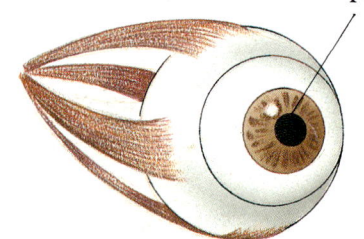

Pupil
Your pupil looks like a black dot in the center of your eye but is in fact a small hole through which light enters. Muscles in the colored part of your eye, the iris, can alter the size of the pupil. It gets bigger in dim light to let in as much light as possible and smaller in bright light, so you do not lose clear vision.

How we see
You see an object when light rays travel from the object into your eyes. Light enters your eye through a small hole, called the pupil. It is focused by the lens at the front of the eye and falls onto a screen at the back of the eye, called the retina. Light-sensitive cells on the retina send information about the image to your brain. At this stage, the image is upside down. Your brain processes the information it receives and turns the image right-side up again.

Rods and cones
There are two types of light-sensitive cells on your retina: rods and cones. Rods work well in dim light, but cannot detect color. Cones are sensitive to color and bright light. The cells get their names because of their shapes.

How do we see in color?
Three types of cone cells allow us to see in color. They detect the three primary colors of light: blue, red, and green. The strength of the signal each type of cone cell sends to your brain determines which colors you see.

Color blindness
Some people cannot see colors properly. Color blindness is caused by faulty or missing cone cells.

About one in twenty people cannot see red and green properly. This is because their retinas are missing the cone cells that register these colors.

FARSIGHTEDNESS AND NEARSIGHTEDNESS

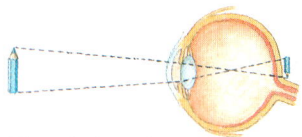

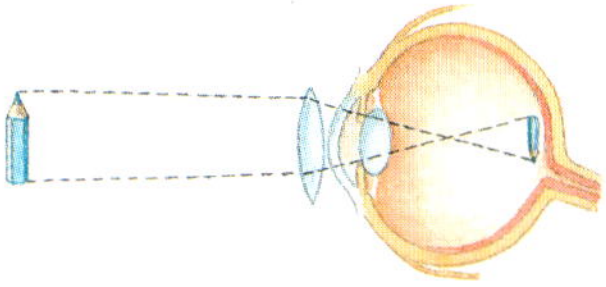

Farsightedness
Being farsighted means you cannot see close objects very clearly. Short eyeballs cause images to fall behind the retina, out of range of sight.

Contact lenses or eyeglasses are worn to correct farsightedness. They make the light rays bend inward, so they are focused onto the retina.

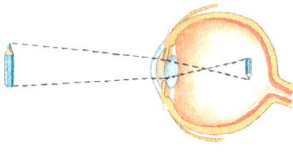

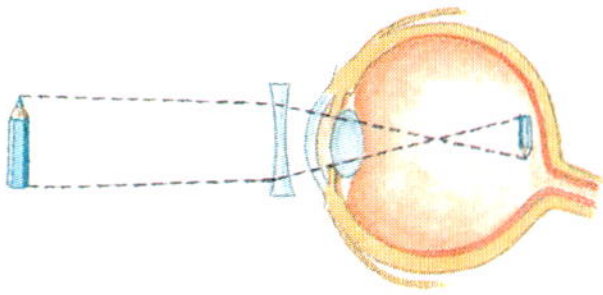

Nearsightedness
Being nearsighted means you cannot see distant objects very clearly. Long eyeballs cause images to fall short, well in front of the retina.

Lenses or eyeglasses worn to correct nearsightedness make light rays bend outward, so they are able to reach the retina.

HOW DO WE KNOW ABOUT OUR EYES?

Roman eye care
Eye diseases, such as cataracts and conjunctivitis, were common in Roman times. **Oculists** set up roadside stands where they sold eye ointments and drops. These often contained herbs, or zinc oxide mixed with honey or gum. Ointments were sold in sticks, stamped with their maker's name.

Opthalmoscope
An opthalmoscope is an instrument used to look inside the eye. A beam of light is directed into the eye to show the surface of the retina. The first opthalmoscope was invented by a German optician, Hermann von Helmholtz, in 1851. Modern versions can be used to detect diseases such as **diabetes** from the state of the blood vessels on the retina.

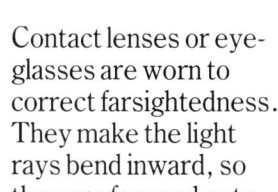

Eyeglasses
Hand-held eyeglasses were used in Venice in the late 13th century. The first contact lenses were developed in the late 19th century. They were made of glass and must have been very uncomfortable!

Laser surgery
Laser beams of ultraviolet light are used in modern eye surgery to reattach detached retinas. They are also being used to correct nearsightedness by shaving layers off the cornea to alter its shape.

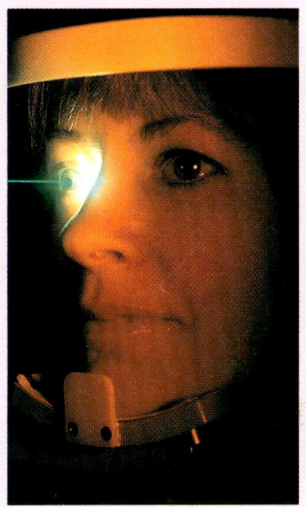

HOW DO WE KNOW
Which Way Is Up?

If you spin around and around in a circle then stop, the chances are that you will feel dizzy or even lose your balance. Your sense of balance is controlled by three semicircular tubes deep inside your ears. You can learn how they work on the next page. Your ears also have another, extremely important job—that of allowing you to hear. Sounds travel from the air deep into your ears. Eventually, the sounds are changed into electrical impulses and sent along a nerve, called the cochlear nerve, to your brain. Your senses of balance and hearing share the same sense organs, but each uses quite different parts of your ears. A second nerve, called the vestibular nerve, carries information about balance from your ear to your brain.

Sound waves
Sound travels through your ears in the form of vibrating waves of air. High-pitched sounds are caused by air vibrating rapidly. Low-pitched sounds are caused by air vibrating slowly.

Hearing aids
There are many reasons why people go deaf, such as ear infections or damaged eardrums. The earliest hearing aids were made from animal horns, designed to collect sound and direct it into the ear. The first electrical hearing aid was invented around 1900. It was bulky and inconvenient. Today, people wear miniature, battery-powered hearing aids that fit neatly behind or even inside their ears.

Hearing aid

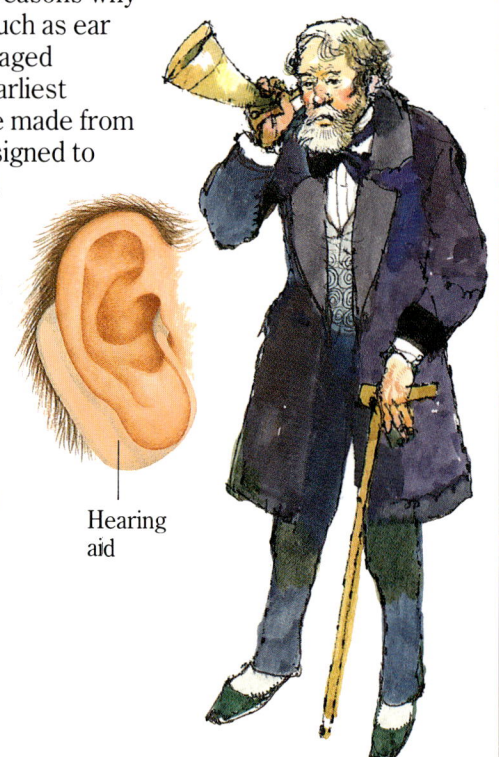

Human   Dolphin   Dog

max 20,000 Hz
max 120,000 Hz
max 35,000 Hz

HEARING RANGES
Your ears are sensitive enough to pick up a wide range of sounds, from the soft sound of a person breathing to the din of a pneumatic drill. The pitch of a sound (how high or low it is) is measured in hertz, or Hz, the number of vibrations per second. Humans can hear sounds between 20–20,000 Hz. Dogs, however, can hear up to 35,000 Hz and dolphins up to 120,000 Hz.

Outer and middle ear
Your outer ear directs sound down a tube, called the auditory canal. Separating the outer and middle ear is a **membrane** called the eardrum. This vibrates when sound hits it. The vibrations are then passed along three tiny bones in the middle ear to another membrane, called the oval window.

Sense of balance
The three semicircular canals, used for balance, branch off from the cochlea. When you turn or tilt your head, fluid in the tubes moves and triggers sensory cells. These send messages to your brain about your new position.

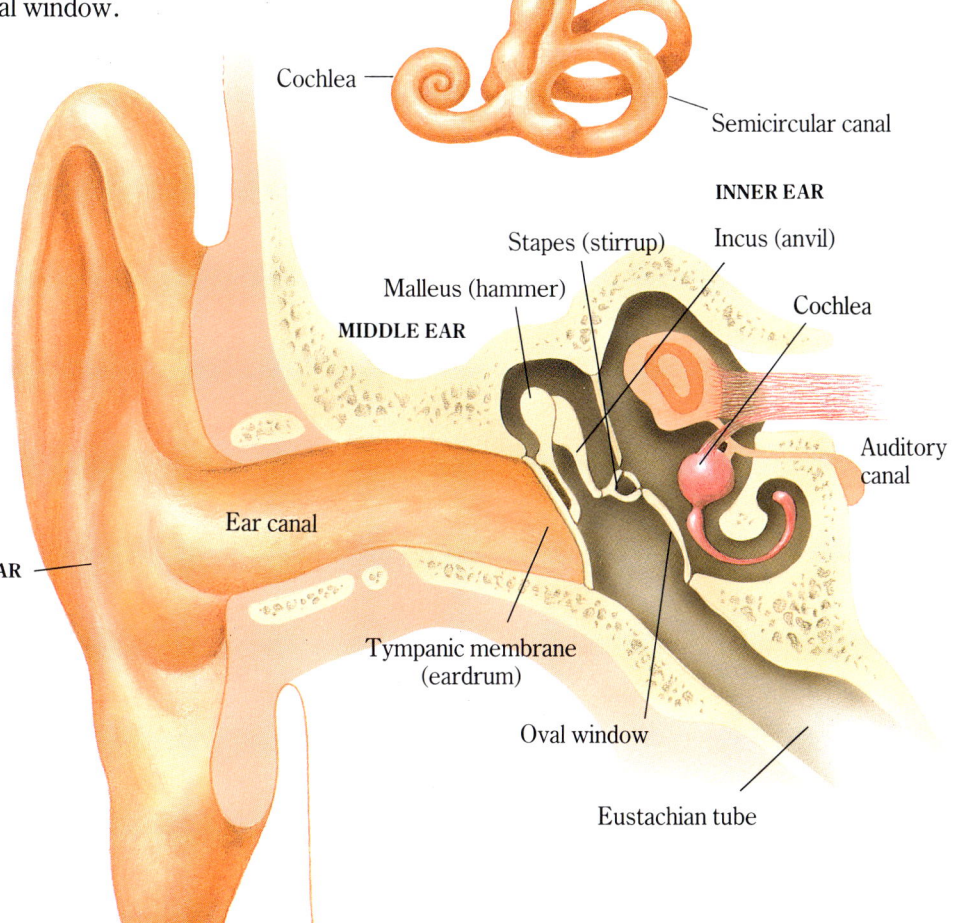

KEEPING BALANCED
You feel dizzy after you've been spinning around because the fluid in the semicircular canals continues to spin. The signals reaching your brain from your ears conflict with those coming from your muscles, which tell your brain that you are, in fact, standing still. Ballet dancers keep their balance by focusing on a fixed spot as they spin. This is called "spotting."

Upside down
The hairs in your semicircular canals are covered with tiny **granules**, which respond to gravity. If you stand on your head, the granules are pulled down by gravity, bending the hairs and sending signals to your brain to tell it you are upside down.

Inner Ear
The vibrations from the oval window are passed on to a coiled, fluid-filled tube called the cochlea, where they make the fluid vibrate. This movement pulls on sensitive hairs lining the tube and triggers electrical impulses, which are sent along the cochlear nerve to your brain.

Eardrum
The eardrum, or tympanic membrane, is stretched across the opening to the middle ear. Sounds hit it and cause it to vibrate. The vibrations are passed along to the three tiny ear bones, or ossicles: the malleus (hammer), incus (anvil), and stapes (stirrup). The stirrup is the smallest bone in your body.

HOW DO WE KNOW
What We Like to Eat?

A quick sniff detects the delicious smell of freshly-baked bread. You immediately feel hungry, and your mouth starts watering. The bread looks tasty, smells tasty, and, as you sink your teeth in, tastes tasty, too! The two main senses involved in telling us if we like what we eat are smell and taste. They work closely together. If food smells strange, it will probably taste horrible. Your sense of taste also tells you how hot or cold food is, so that you don't burn your tongue.

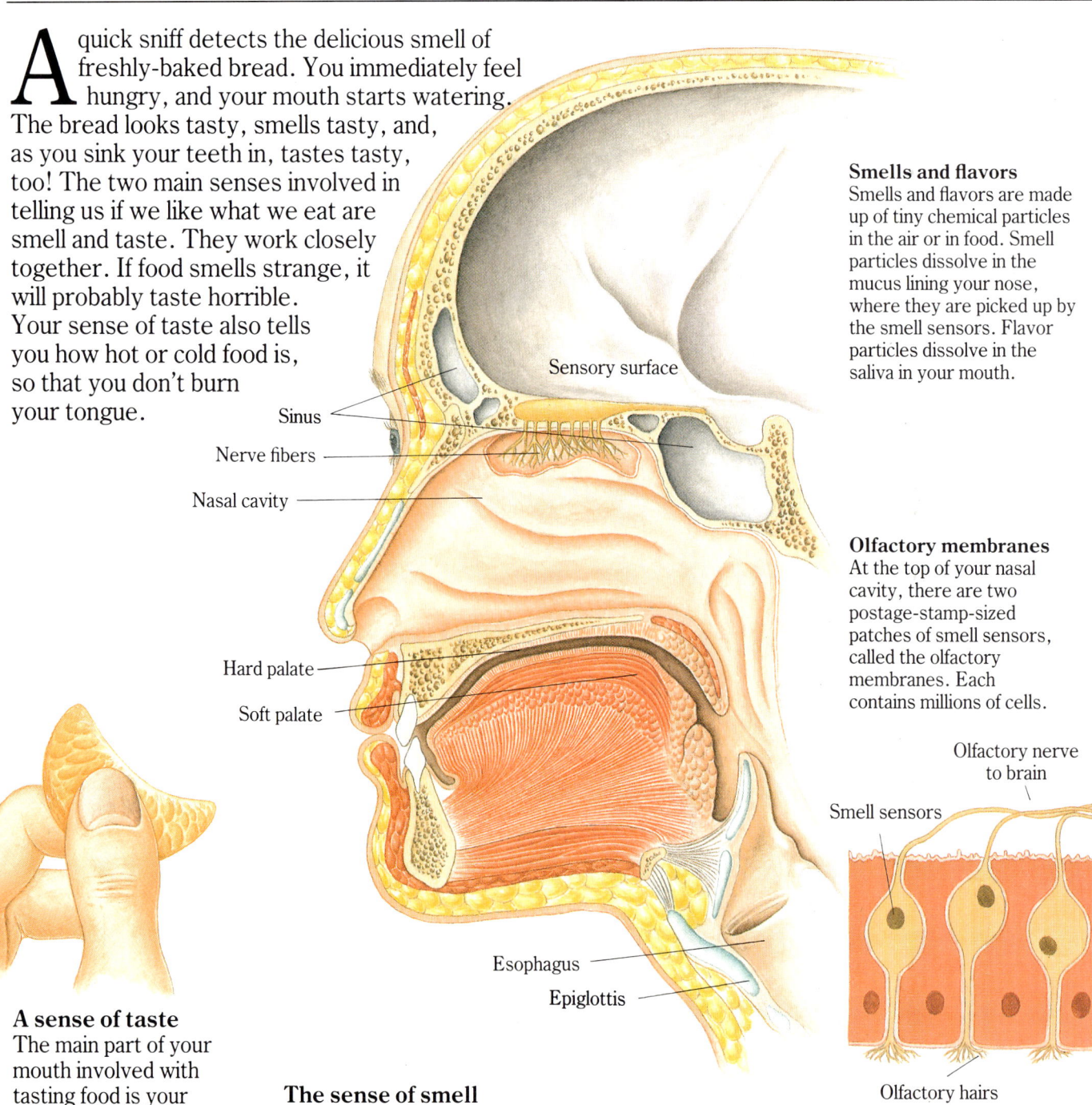

Smells and flavors
Smells and flavors are made up of tiny chemical particles in the air or in food. Smell particles dissolve in the mucus lining your nose, where they are picked up by the smell sensors. Flavor particles dissolve in the saliva in your mouth.

Olfactory membranes
At the top of your nasal cavity, there are two postage-stamp-sized patches of smell sensors, called the olfactory membranes. Each contains millions of cells.

Inside the nasal cavity
Each smell sensor has a tiny hair attached to it that waves around in the lining of mucus inside your nose. The hairs pick up smells that entered with the air and dissolved in the mucus.

A sense of taste
The main part of your mouth involved with tasting food is your tongue, which is covered in thousands of flavor-sensitive taste buds (see right). Your tongue also helps to mash and soften your food to make it easier to swallow and digest.

The sense of smell
When you breathe in, smells in the air travel up your nose and into a hollow space called your nasal cavity. The smells are picked up by sensory cells. There are about 14 different types of these cells, each of which detects a different kind of smell. Signals are then sent along the olfactory nerve to your brain. You get a stronger signal when you sniff because you draw air higher into your nasal cavity and closer to the sensory cells.

GOOD AND BAD SMELLS

The human nose can detect about 10,000 smells, most of which are combinations of different smell particles. Our sense of smell develops very quickly. Experiments have shown that babies at the age of just six days can tell the difference between their mother's smell and the smell of strangers. Pleasant smells include the scent of flowers and the smell of fresh food. But even unpleasant smells have their uses. The smell of spoiled food warns you that it might be harmful to eat. The smell of something burning warns you of the danger of fire.

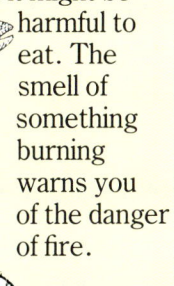

Tastes on the tongue

The surface of your tongue is covered with clusters of minute, taste-sensitive cells, called taste buds. They pick up flavor particles dissolved in the saliva in your mouth. They then send signals about what you have tasted to your brain. Your taste buds can only detect four basic flavors: sweet, sour, salty, and bitter. Combinations of these flavors make your food tasty. Your sense of smell also helps to pick up more subtle tastes. So, if you have a cold, and your nose is blocked up, all your food may seem to taste the same.

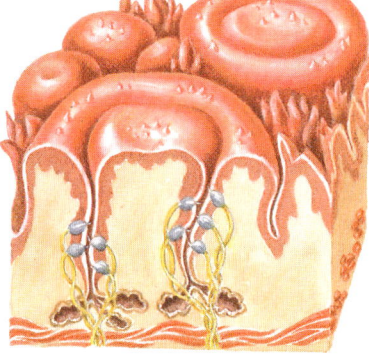

Taste buds

Through the tongue

Taste buds are embedded into the surface of the tongue, on and between tiny bumps called papillae. The papillae come in three different shapes, each responsible for detecting different flavors.

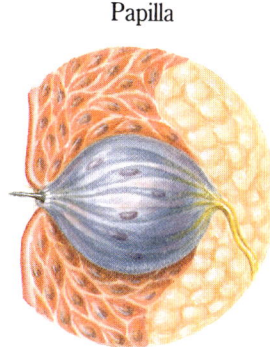

Papilla

A taste bud

A taste bud is a group of about 30 sensitive cells, arranged much like the segments of an orange. The individual cells are long and slender. A hole at the top of the "orange" lets the flavor particles into the taste bud.

Avoiding smells

In the past people used to carry small bouquets of flowers to ward off bad smells.

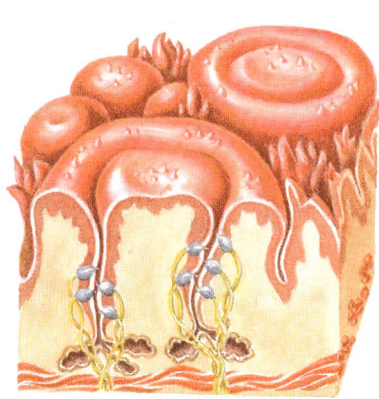

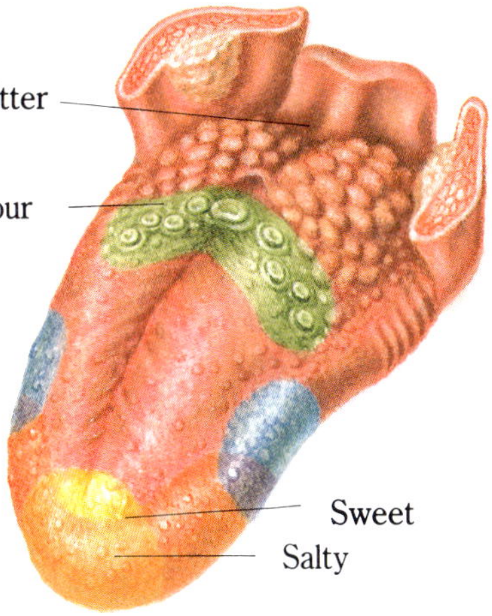

Taste areas

The four basic tastes are detected on different areas of your tongue, as shown above. The back of your tongue detects bitter flavors, the tip salty flavors, and the sides sweet and sour flavors.

BEING SICK

One of the surest ways of discovering that you didn't like what you ate is being sick. Half-digested food is rejected by your stomach and forced back up.

27

HOW DO WE KNOW
Germs Make Us Sick?

Most of the illnesses we contract, from coughs and colds to potentially fatal diseases, such as dysentery and even AIDS, are caused by tiny living things, commonly known as germs. Germs may be bacteria, viruses, **protozoa**, or **fungi**. There are thousands of different kinds of germs, each responsible for a different kind of illness. Germs enter your body in the air you breathe and through cuts or scratches. Once inside, they multiply and stop your cells from functioning properly. Your body reacts by showing the symptoms of the illness, such as a temperature, nausea, aches and pains, and so on. Centuries ago, however, doctors had no idea what germs were or how they affected the body. They had other ideas about how illnesses spread.

Early ideas
The ancient Greeks believed that illnesses were caused by an imbalance of the four humors (see page 4). In the Middle Ages, the devil was held responsible.

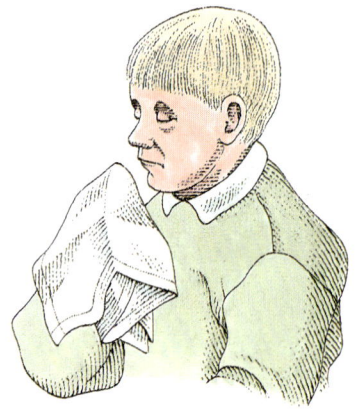

Airborne attack
Louis Pasteur (below left) was the first to realize that germs were carried through the air. Before this, people believed in "spontaneous generation." They thought that germs were made by the objects on which they appeared.

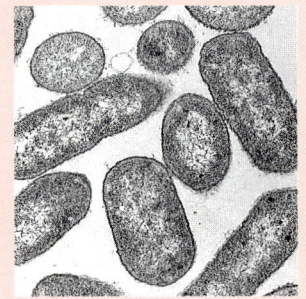

Microscopic menaces
Germs are too small to see except under a microscope. Van Leeuwenhoek studied bacteria under his early microscope in 1683 but had no idea of the relationship between germs and disease.

LOUIS PASTEUR
Louis Pasteur (1822–1895) was the first person to suspect that germs were responsible for causing illness. A brilliant French chemist and biologist, Pasteur's first experiments were concerned with the bacteria that turned beer and milk sour. He discovered that these germs could be killed by heat, in a process now known as pasteurization. Pasteur went on to conclude that bacteria could also cause things to go wrong with the human body, although some bacteria are harmless or even useful. He published his theory of germ disease in 1865.

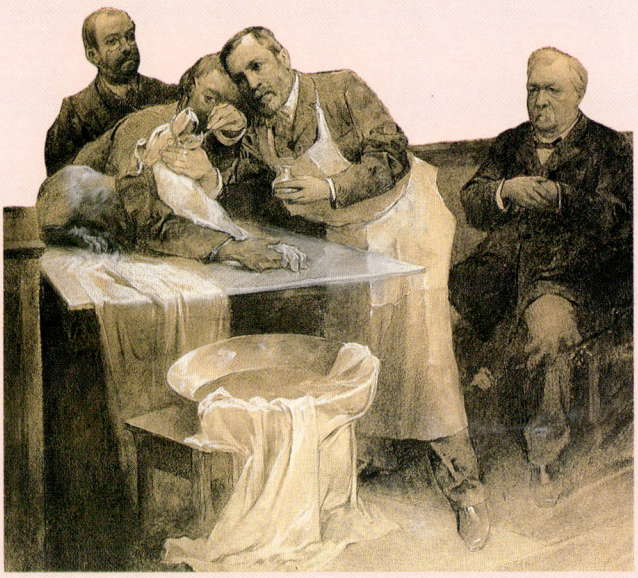

Antiseptics to the rescue
One of the side effects of Pasteur's work on germs was the discovery of antiseptics by the British doctor Joseph Lister (1827–1912). Until that time, patients often died from gangrene or blood poisoning after operations, because their wounds became infected. Lister realized that it was necessary to kill airborne germs before they could reach the wound. He could not use heat to kill germs, as Pasteur had done, but found that a solution of carbolic acid did the job just as well. As a result of Lister's work, surgery became much safer.

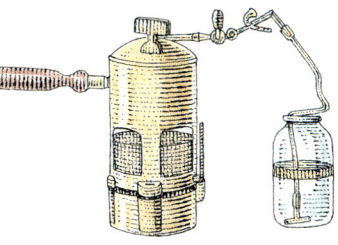

Antiseptic spray
Lister used the equipment shown above to spray carbolic acid onto the patient and into the air around an operating table.

Safe surgery
Lister performed the first operation using antiseptics in 1867. Modern surgical instruments and operating rooms are sterilized to kill germs.

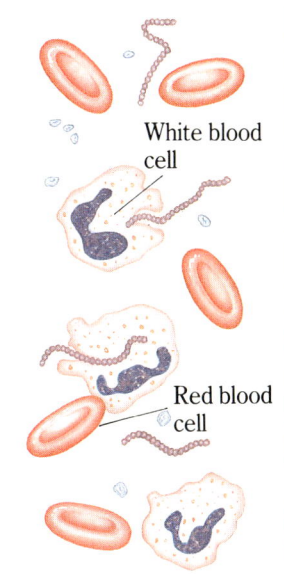

White blood cell

Red blood cell

SELF DEFENSE
Your body has an **immune system** that protects it from attack by germs. The white cells in your blood are the most important part of this system. One type of white blood cell, called lymphocytes, makes chemicals called antibodies, which attach themselves to germs and kill them. Another type of white blood cell, called phagocytes, surrounds germs and destroys them.

AIDS
AIDS, or Acquired Immune Deficiency Syndrome, is one of the most serious illnesses facing the world today. It is caused by a virus, called HIV (Human Immunodeficiency Virus). This virus destroys the body's immune system, leaving people at serious risk from diseases they would normally be able to fight off.

HOW DO WE KNOW
How We Get Better?

If you are sick, and if your body's own immune system cannot fight off the infection, you will probably pay a visit to a doctor. He or she will examine you, identify the problem, and make a diagnosis. You may then be given medicine to help you get better or be sent to a hospital for further tests. In addition to this type of "conventional" medicine, there is also a branch of "alternative" medicine in which herbal remedies, for example, may be used instead of drugs to treat people.

For centuries, illnesses were studied with great interest, and doctors tried to cure people who were sick, but very little attention was paid to preventing illness in the first place. Preventative medicine grew in importance in the late 18th century. It is now widely practiced throughout the world.

Herbal medicine
Herbs and plants have been used for thousands of years for their medicinal properties. Herbal medicine is still the main form of treatment among tribes in the Amazon rain forest, for example, although local knowledge is being lost as the forests are destroyed. Some important modern drugs originally come from plants, such as aspirin (from willow bark), and digitalis, a drug found in foxglove flowers and used to treat heart disease.

Witch doctors
In some tribal societies, traditional healers, or shamans, take the place of doctors. They perform healing ceremonies in which they ask the help of spirits in curing the sick and wounded.

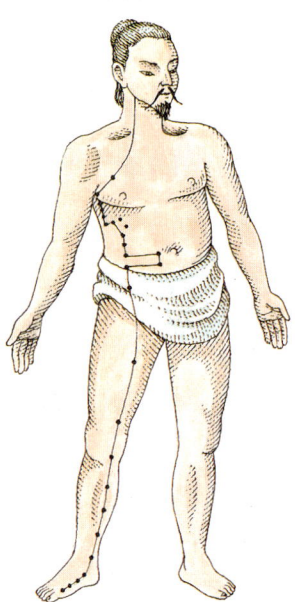

Acupuncture
Acupuncture is an ancient Chinese treatment first used about 5,000 years ago. Needles are inserted into **pressure points** along special channels carrying the life force, *T'chi*, through the body.

Dr. Hippocrates
Hippocrates (about 460–377 B.C.) ran a famous medical school on the Greek island of Kos. His teaching laid the foundations of modern medicine, and his guidelines for doctors are still followed today.

Sweet dreams
In Roman times, sick people spent the night in the temple of Aesculpius, the god of healing. They believed the god would visit them in their dreams and tell them how to get better.

JENNER AND VACCINATION

One of the most important breakthroughs in preventative medicine came with Edward Jenner's discovery of a smallpox vaccine in 1796. At the time, smallpox was a widespread and much-feared disease all over the world. Jenner (1749–1823), a British country doctor, found that dairymaids who had had cowpox (a mild form of smallpox) never caught smallpox. He inoculated a small boy, James Phipps, with a dose of cowpox and then later with smallpox. The cowpox vaccine did its job, and the boy did not develop smallpox.

Rabies vaccine

Rabies is a potentially fatal disease transmitted from animals to humans through infected saliva (usually from a dog bite). It can cause fits, foaming at the mouth, and death within four or five days. A rabies vaccine was discovered by Louis Pasteur (see page 28) in 1885.

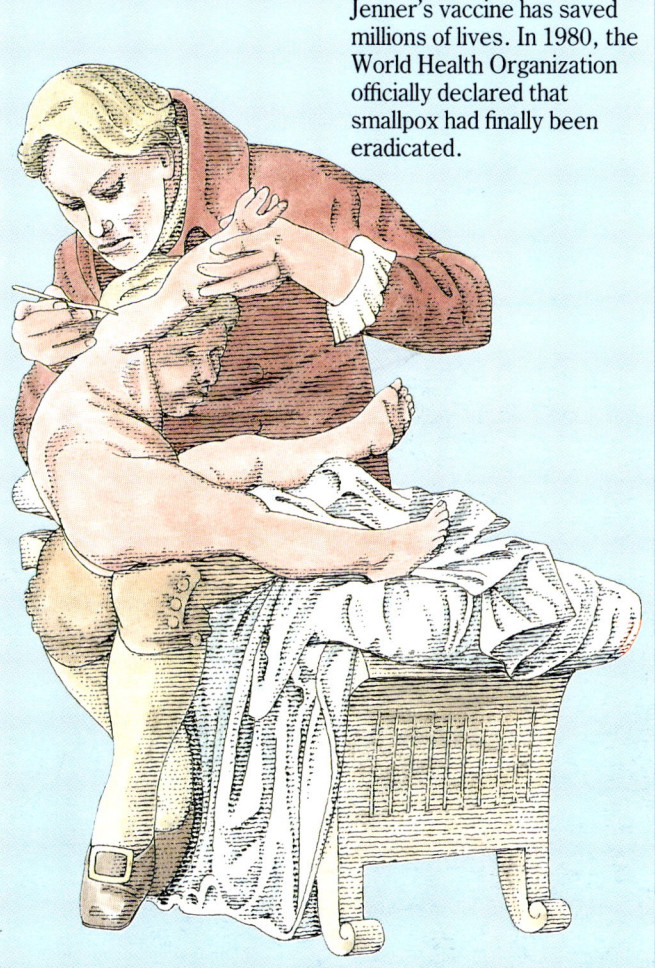

Jenner's vaccine has saved millions of lives. In 1980, the World Health Organization officially declared that smallpox had finally been eradicated.

IMMUNIZATION IN PROGRESS

Your lymphocytes (white blood cells) automatically produce antibodies to kill particular germs.

To immunize you against a particular disease, you are given a small dose of the germs that cause it.

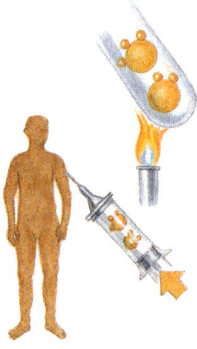

Your body is fooled into thinking it is under attack and produces the correct antibodies to kill the germs.

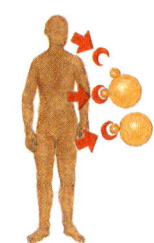

This makes you resistant, or immune, to the disease before you have actually caught it.

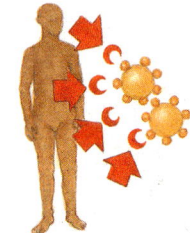

The discovery of penicillin

Antibiotics, including penicillin, are widely used today to treat diseases caused by bacteria. Penicillin was discovered in 1928 by accident. Alexander Fleming (1881–1955) returned from vacation to find mold growing on a dish of bacteria in his laboratory. The mold, called penicillium, had begun to kill the bacteria. The antibiotic that was obtained from the mold was called penicillin.

Treatment by chemicals

One of the greatest influences on Fleming was the German scientist, Paul Ehrlich (1854–1915). Ehrlich was awarded the Nobel Prize for Medicine in 1908 for his work on immunity. Then he began his pioneering work on the use of laboratory-made chemicals, rather than drugs derived from animals or plants, to treat diseases. This practice is called chemotherapy. Today, chemotherapy is also used to treat diseases, such as cancers, that are not caused by germs.

Modern drugs

Today, a vast range of drugs is used to treat illnesses. Most are made in laboratories, such as drugs like aspirin, which originally came from plants. Many drugs are only available by prescription, which means they are only dispensed under doctor's orders.

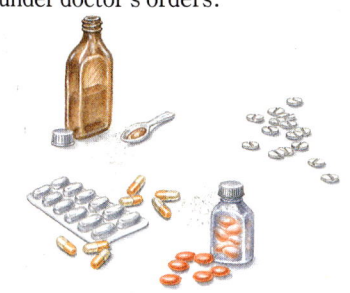

HOW DO WE KNOW
What's Inside Us?

Early anatomists (scientists who study the structure of the body) were rarely allowed to dissect human bodies (see pages 4–5). Instead, they had to rely on animal dissections to further their studies. They then applied what they discovered to the human body. Needless to say, guesswork played a large part in their theories! Some doctors, such as Galen, were more fortunate. He worked as a surgeon to the Roman gladiators and had plenty of opportunity for investigating wounds, broken bones, and so on. Today, doctors and surgeons have a wide range of highly sophisticated technology and equipment for looking inside us.

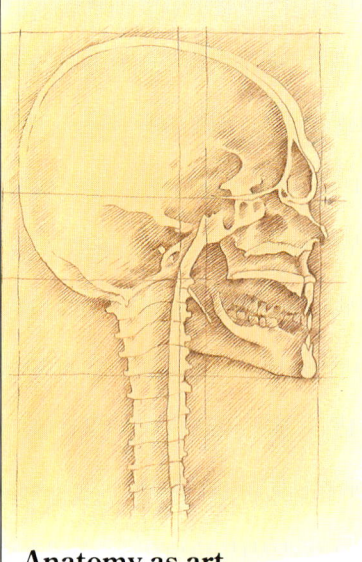

Anatomy as art
The great Italian painter, Leonardo da Vinci (1452–1519), studied the human body closely and made some amazingly detailed drawings of its anatomy.

In 1632 Rembrandt painted *The Anatomy Lecture of Dr. Nicolaes Tulp*. Dr. Tulp was a respected physician and surgeon. The body is that of an executed criminal.

Tools of the trade
From the ancient Egyptians to the Romans to the present day, scalpels have been traditional tools of the surgeon's trade. Tweezers and saws have also been used throughout history.

THE X-RAY MYSTERY
Today, X rays are taken for granted as a means of looking inside the body. But X rays were only discovered in 1895, by a German physicist, Wilhelm Roentgen (1845–1923). During an experiment, he noticed that certain invisible rays of energy could pass through flesh but not through denser bones. He called the rays "X" rays because of their mysterious nature.

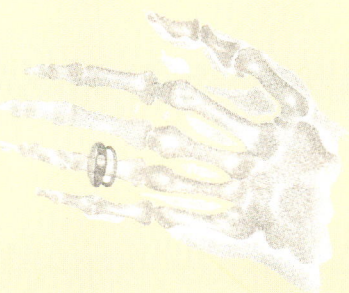

The first X-ray picture ever taken was of Roentgen's wife's hand. X rays are used to detect broken bones, tumors, and other abnormalities inside the body.

Modern techniques
The equipment used today for looking inside the body and performing surgery is extremely advanced. Much of it has been made possible because of the advances in technology in the last 50 years. Such developments as CAT (computerized axial tomographic) scanners (right), ultrasound scanners, and lasers have allowed doctors to examine the insides of the body without having to cut it open. This is far safer and less traumatic for the patient.

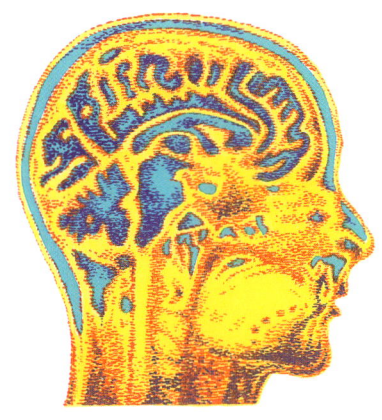

Magnetic resonance image
In magnetic resonance imaging (MRI), a person is surrounded by a powerful magnetic field and their body's response recorded as an image. This system can show even soft tissues in great detail.

◀ Endoscopes
An endoscope is a long, tubelike instrument inserted into a patient to examine his or her insides. Endoscopes can carry lasers or miniature surgical instruments for performing surgery inside the body.

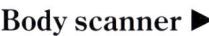

Body scanner ▶
The first whole body scanner was developed in 1973 by a team of British scientists. The patient's body is scanned by a rotating X-ray machine, the findings are fed into a computer, and an image is produced on a screen.

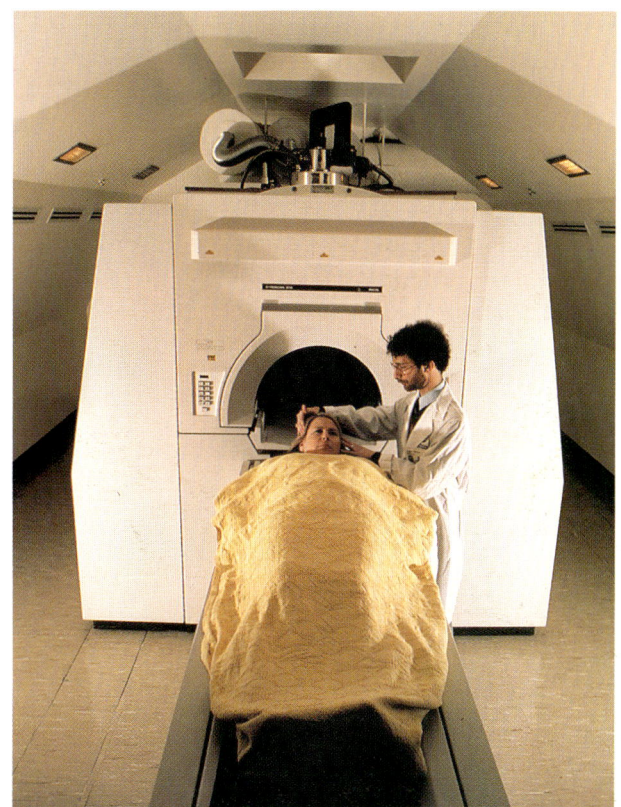

HOW DO WE KNOW
Where We Come From?

Today we know that, in order for a baby to form and grow inside its mother, two cells need to join together. These are a sperm from the father and an ovum (egg) from the mother. In the past, however, people had different ideas about where we come from. Aristotle believed that it was the male sperm alone that created and formed the fetus from the female's blood. Harvey recognized that an ovum was needed but still believed in the sperm as the creative force. Toward the end of the 17th century, the ancient theory of "preformation" became popular. Its followers believed that a baby began life as a miniature version of an adult, with all its body parts already formed. It only had to grow bigger.

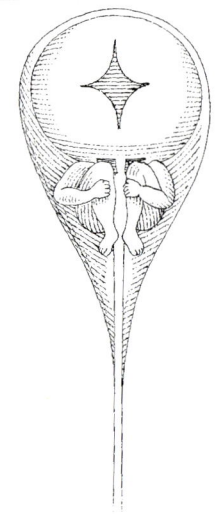

Beginnings of life
This drawing, by the 17th-century Dutch scientist, Hartsoeker, shows a little human already formed in miniature, crouching inside a sperm.

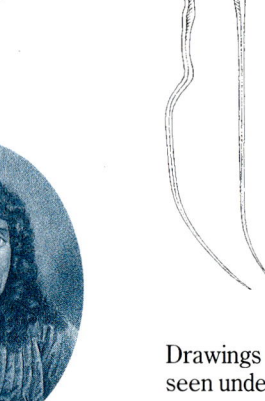

Drawings of sperm as seen under a 17th-century microscope

Under the microscope
Van Leeuwenhoek saw and studied sperm under his microscope as early as 1677. But the ovum was not discovered until 1827 and fertilization not observed under the microscope until the late 19th century.

A BABY BEGINS

For a baby to be produced, an egg and a sperm cell must join together in a process called fertilization. This can happen after a man and woman have had sexual intercourse. Sperm from the man's penis enter the woman's vagina and swim up through her womb and into her egg ducts. If they meet an egg, one of them may fertilize it.

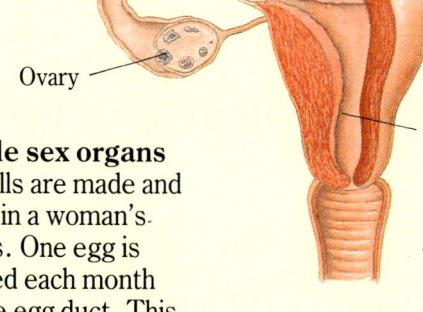

Female sex organs
Egg cells are made and stored in a woman's ovaries. One egg is released each month into the egg duct. This is called ovulation.

If the egg is not fertilized the woman has a "period." The bloody lining of the womb, which would hold a fertilized egg, breaks down and passes out of her body.

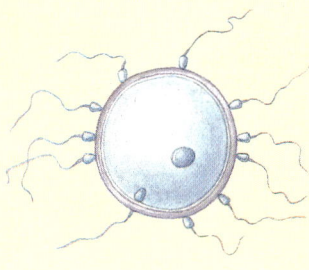

Many sperm cluster around the egg, but only one can break through and fertilize it. The rest die.

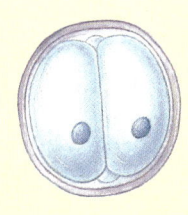

The egg and sperm join together to form a new cell. It divides in two, then into four, and so on until it forms a ball of 64 individual cells.

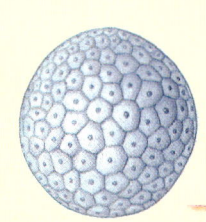

The ball of cells travels down the egg duct and embeds itself in the lining of the mother's womb.

Here it grows and develops over the next nine months into a baby.

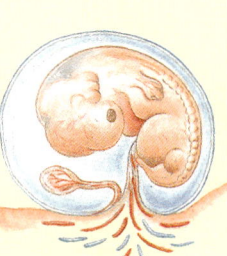

GRADUAL GROWTH

The German scientist, Karl Wolff (1733–1794), rejected the theory of preformation. He believed a human being developed from a simple structure, with no preformed organs or body parts, into a baby ready to be born. It was not until the 19th century, with the discovery that cells form the building blocks of living things, that the theory of preformation was finally rejected.

Male sex organs

Sperm cells are produced inside a man's testicles. They travel along two tubes into the penis. A man produces millions of sperm every day. The ancient Chinese believed that sperm were made in a man's right kidney!

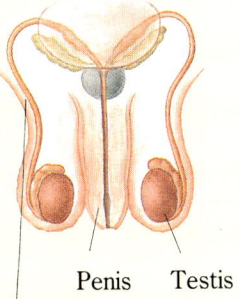

Penis   Testis

Sperm duct

Gene generation

In its cells, a developing baby contains instructions that will determine what it will look like (its hair and eye color and so on), its blood group, and other characteristics. These instructions are called genes. They are passed from parents to children in a process called heredity.

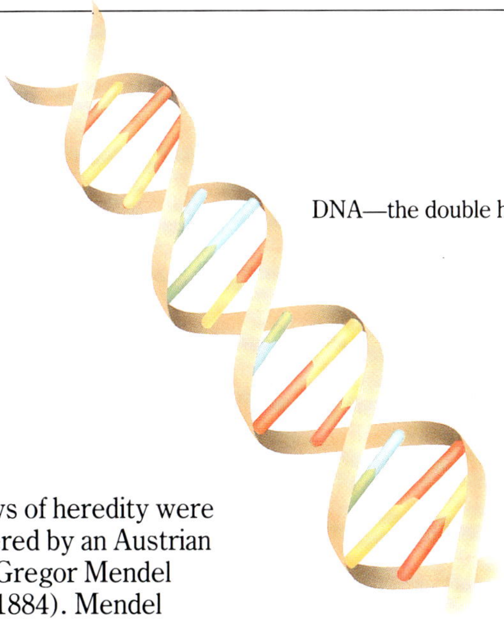

The laws of heredity were discovered by an Austrian monk, Gregor Mendel (1822–1884). Mendel conducted an experiment using pea plants to see how features, such as color and size, are passed from one generation to another.

Chromosomes

Chromosomes are tiny, threadlike structures in your cells, made up of thousands of genes. You inherit 23 chromosomes from each of your parents. Sex chromosomes determine whether you are born male or female.

Whose hair?

Each parent contributes a gene for hair color. Some genes exercise more control over a characteristic than others. They are known as dominant genes. The genes that exercise less control over a characteristic are called recessive. Genes for dark hair are dominant over genes for fair hair.

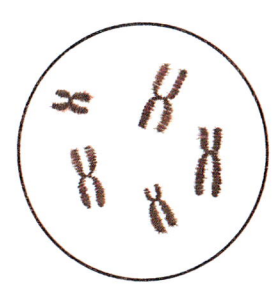

DNA—the double helix

DNA

Genes are made up of a complicated chemical called DNA (deoxyribonucleic acid). DNA looks like a twisted ladder. The order of the rungs of the ladder, and the chemicals in them, varies to form a code of instructions for a particular body feature. The structure of DNA was discovered in 1953 by Francis Crick and James Watson. It is known as a double helix.

Father   Mother

Has genes for brown hair and genes for fair hair   Has genes for fair hair only

Fair hair   Brown hair   Brown hair   Fair hair

HOW DO WE KNOW
About Hormones?

Apart from the electrical signals carried by your nerve cells, there is another set of messages traveling around your body. They are carried by chemicals, called hormones, which are released from **glands** into your bloodstream. Each type of hormone controls a different part of the body or a different body process. This whole system is called the endocrine system. When hormones were first discovered in the 19th century, they were called "internal secretions." It was not until 1906 that they were given the name *hormones*. This comes from the Greek word *homaein*, which means stimulating or driving.

Hormone history
In 1830, a German scientist, Johannes Muller, suggested that there might be special glands in the body secreting fluids into the bloodstream. But his suspicions were not backed up by experiments until Arnold Berthold did his pioneering experiments on bird hormones in 1849.

Von Mering and Minkowski
In 1889, another breakthrough in the study of hormones (endocrinology) occurred. During a series of experiments on dogs, two German doctors, Von Mering and Minkowski, discovered the link between the pancreas and sugar levels in the blood (see right).

Brain
Your brain controls the production and release of hormones into your bloodstream. Some hormones, such as those affecting growth, work quite slowly. Others, such as adrenalin, act in seconds.

Thyroid gland
Your thyroid gland regulates your metabolism (the use of energy by your body).

Parathyroid glands
The four tiny parathyroids, located behind the thyroid gland, produce parathormone, which controls the level of calcium in your bones and blood.

Adrenal glands
Your adrenal glands produce several different hormones, including adrenalin (see page 37).

Pancreas
The pancreas produces the hormone insulin, which regulates the sugar level in your blood. Lack of insulin can cause the disease diabetes (see right).

Testicles
A man's testicles produce the male sex hormone, testosterone. It controls how men's bodies develop.

Pituitary gland
The pea-sized pituitary gland hangs by a stalk from your brain. It is your master gland, controlling 11 other glands as well as producing its own hormones, such as growth hormone.

Ovaries
A woman's ovaries produce the female sex hormones, estrogen and progesterone. They control how women's bodies develop and grow.

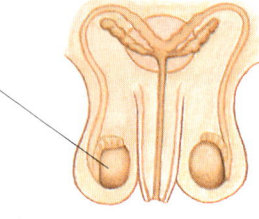

Milk production

The pituitary gland produces two hormones, called oxytocin and prolactin, which control the production and flow of a mother's milk after she has had a baby. The action of a baby sucking on its mother's nipple triggers the pituitary into releasing these particular hormones.

Insulin and diabetes

The hormone insulin, produced by the pancreas, controls the level of sugar in your blood. This provides energy for cells. A lack of insulin can lead to diabetes, with a wide range of symptoms, including weight loss, tiredness, and even cataracts. Diabetes sufferers have to have regular injections of insulin. Today, human insulin is genetically engineered in laboratories. Earlier, insulin from cows and pigs was used. Insulin was not discovered in the body until 1922.

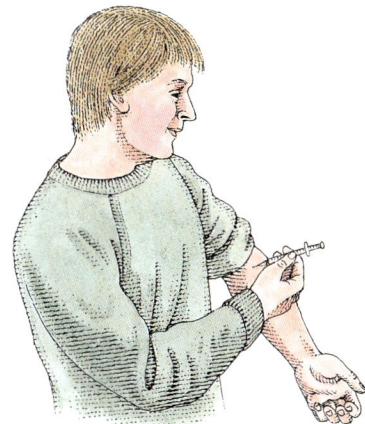

Hair and skin

Sex hormones are produced in large quantities when you reach the age of puberty (about age 11 for girls and age 13 for boys). The changing levels of testosterone especially can cause problems, including acne. It is thought that sex hormones may also be partly responsible for baldness in men later in life.

FIGHT OR FLIGHT?

When you are frightened, adrenalin automatically pours from your adrenal glands into your bloodstream. It speeds up your heart rate, quickens your breathing, and prepares your muscles for action. Your body is put on the alert so that you can either stay and fight your way out of danger or flee. A similar reaction happens when you are angry or excited.

RATES OF GROWTH

The growth hormone, somatotropin, is produced by your pituitary gland. If too little of the growth hormone is made, a person may grow very little. Too much hormone can cause a person to grow much taller than normal. You tend to grow slightly faster at night, when more somatotropin is released into your blood system.

HOW DO WE KNOW
We Are Getting Older?

Your body changes throughout your life. From birth, you grow taller and stronger until you are about 18–20 years old. As a child, you grow very quickly when you are two years old and again when you are ten. In your early teens, you enter adolescence, during which you change from a child into an adult. Your body changes in many ways. Girls begin to grow breasts and to have periods. Boys grow more hair on their faces and bodies, and their voices change and get deeper. From then on, your body stays about the same until your late middle age and old age. As people reach old age, their bodies become more frail, and it takes longer for them to repair themselves. Their skin becomes more wrinkled, and their hair may go gray or white. But it's not all doom and gloom! With healthier diets and life-styles, people are living longer than ever before in many parts of the world.

COLD AND OLD
Aristotle believed that old age was a result of the body cooling down. Warming and cooling were important parts of his theories on the human body.

Outward signs
The main signs that time is passing and that you are getting older are outward ones. Wrinkled skin is caused by the skin losing its elastic quality and sagging. Gray hair occurs when the amount of the coloring pigment, melanin, gets less and less until there is none left. Older people also seem to shrink in height. This is because the cartilage discs between their vertebrae shrink, and their spines get shorter.

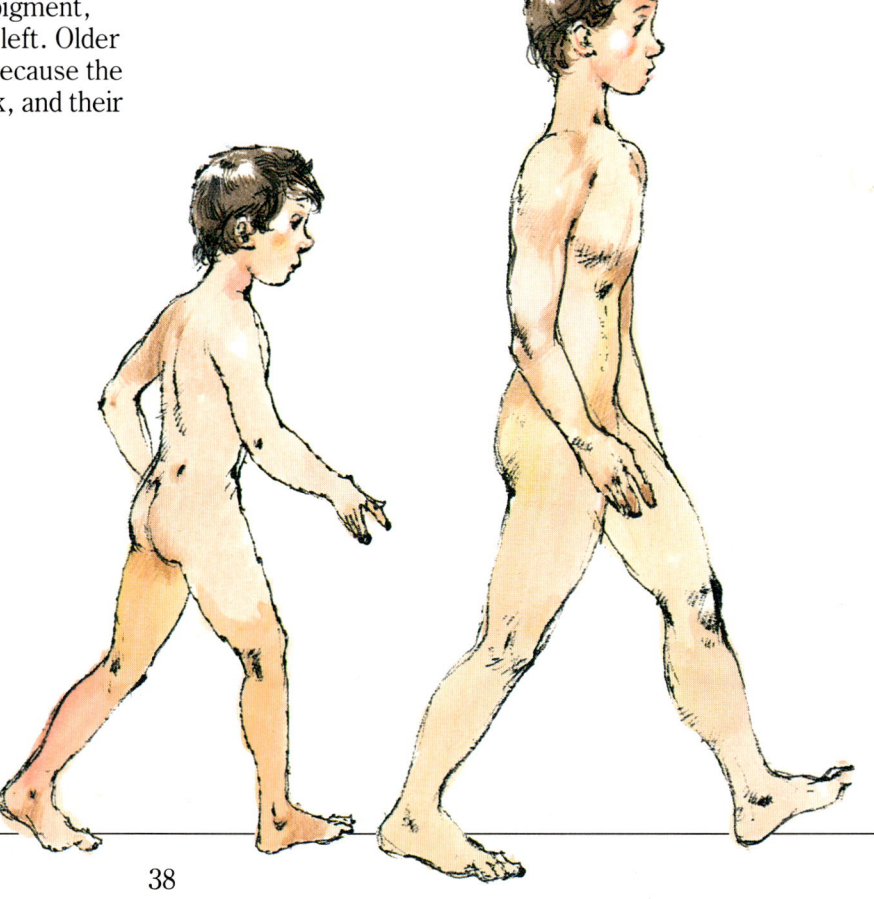

KEEPING HEALTHY, LIVING LONGER

Keep fit ▶
Regular exercise is an important part of staying healthy. It strengthens your muscles, heart, and lungs, as well as helping you stay slim and relaxed.

◀ Healthy eating
A balanced diet and sensible eating will provide you with all the ingredients you need for good health without making you too fat. Being overweight can cause heart disease and other kinds of illnesses.

Staying well ▶
Your health can be greatly improved by looking after your body. Smoking and drinking too much alcohol can seriously damage your health.

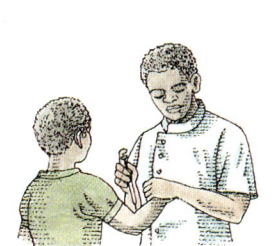

Life expectancy is the average number of years a person can expect to live.

LIFE EXPECTANCY
In Western countries, in particular, people are living longer as a result of better health care and diets. Two hundred years ago, the average life expectancy for men was 47 years and for women 51 years. Today it is 73 and 76 years. In poorer countries, life spans are improving, but people are still at greater risk from disease, poor living conditions, and food shortages.

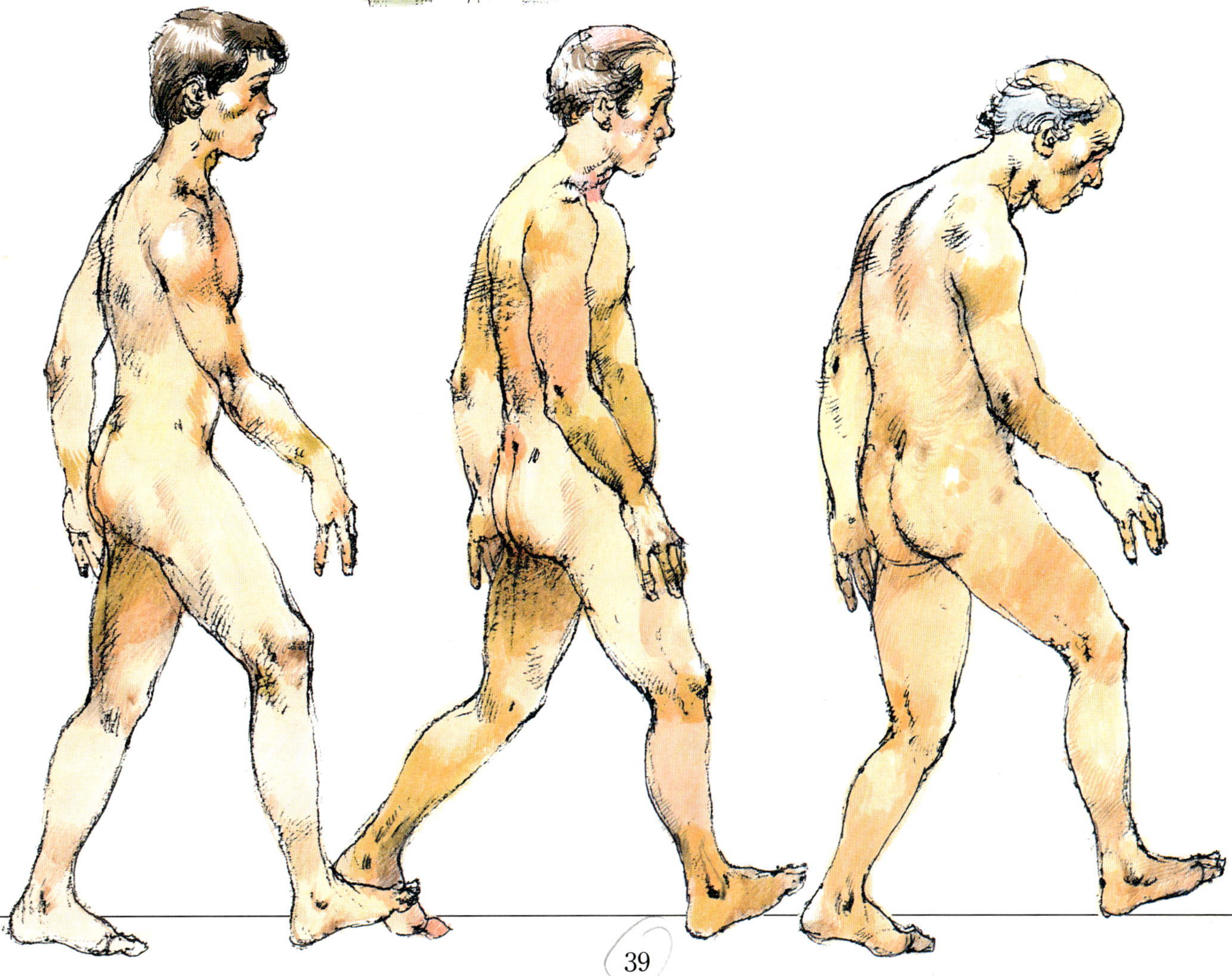

Glossary

Anatomist
A scientist who studies the structure of the body, often by dissection

Anesthetics
Drugs used to stop patients from feeling pain or discomfort during an operation

Bone marrow
The jellylike substance inside bones that makes new red blood cells

Central nervous system
The brain and spinal cord

Chemist
A scientist who studies chemistry

Circulation
The way in which the blood flows through the body in a continuous path, pumped by the heart

Diabetes
A disease caused by a lack of the hormone insulin, which controls the level of sugar in the blood

Electrodes
Metal sensors attached to a person's head to monitor the electrical activity of their brain

Electrons
Tiny particles inside atoms, with a negative electrical charge

Enzymes
Proteins, made in the cells of organisms, that speed up chemical reactions

Fungi
The group of living things that includes toadstools, molds, and yeasts. Some fungi cause diseases in humans.

Glands
Groups of cells that produce hormones and other secretions

Granules
Tiny grains or particles

Hormones
Chemicals carried in the bloodstream to various parts of the body, which they control

Immune system
The body's natural defense mechanism against diseases. Its main weapons are white blood cells, which kill disease-carrying germs.

Membrane
A thin sheet of tissue

Nerves
A system of cells (neurons) that carry information from the body to the brain, and vice versa, in the form of electrical signals

Nutrients
Substances in food that the body needs to function and stay healthy

Nutritionists
Scientists who study food, the nourishment it contains, and the effect it has on the body

Oculist
A specialist in eye diseases

Organs
Body parts, such as the heart, lungs, liver, and kidneys, made of different types of cells

Peripheral nervous system
The nerves that run to the arms, legs, eyes, ears, and so on

Physician
A doctor or surgeon

Pressure points
In acupuncture, invisible points along invisible meridian lines running through the body. These lines carry the life force, *T'chi*.

Protozoa
Microscopic, single-celled organisms, which can cause diseases

Sensory receptors
Nerve cells in the skin, which detect sensations such as light touch, pain, pressure, and temperature changes

Spinal cord
The bundle of nerves running down the middle of the spine

Tissues
Groups of cells of the same type that do a specific job in the body. Skin and muscles are types of tissue.

Tourniquet
A band or strap tied tightly around an arm or leg to stop the blood from flowing into the limb through the arteries

Transfusions
In a blood transfusion, the exchange of blood for a new supply

Valves
Flaps of skin in the heart or veins that close to prevent blood from flowing the wrong way

Index

A
acupuncture 30
adolescence 38
adrenal glands 36–37
aging 38–39
AIDS 29
alveoli 14
anatomists 6, 32
anesthetics 20
antibiotics 31
antiseptics 29
aorta 11, 13
Aristotle 4, 18, 34, 38
arteries 11, 12

B
babies 34, 37
bacteria 28, 31
balance, sense of 24, 25
ball-and-socket joints 7
Berthold, Arnold 36
blood 10–13, 29
body scanners 33
brain 5, 18–19, 21, 22, 24, 36
breathing 14–15
Broca, Paul 18

C
calories 16
cancers 31
capillaries 11
cells 4–5, 19, 34–35, 39
    blood cells 10, 29
chemotherapy 31
chromosomes 35
color vision 23
contact lenses 23
cranium 7
Crick, Francis 35

D
deafness 24
diabetes 37
diet 16, 39
digestive system 17
diseases *see* illnesses
dissection 4, 32
DNA 35
drugs 30, 31

E
ears 24–25
Ehrlich, Paul 31
Eijkmann, Christiaan 17
electroencephalographs (EEG) 19
electron microscopes 5
endoscopes 33
esophagus 17
eyeglasses 23
eyes 22–23

F
face 9
femoral artery 11
Fleming, Alexander 31
food 16–17, 26–27, 39

G
Galen 8, 12, 13, 14, 15, 16, 32
Gall, Franz Joseph 19
Galvani, Luigi 9
genes 35
germs 28–29
glands 36–37
Greeks, ancient 4, 8, 19, 28, 30
growth 37, 38

H
hair 37, 38
Harvey, William 12, 13
healthiness 39
hearing 24–25
heart 9, 11, 12–13
herbal medicine 30
heredity 35
Hippocrates 30
Hooke, Robert 5, 15
hormones 36–37
humors 4, 28

I
illnesses 17, 23, 28–31, 37, 39
immune system, 29
immunization 31
insulin 37
intestines 17
invertebrates 6

J
Jenner, Edward 31
joints 7
jugular vein 11

L
Laënnec, René 13
Landsteiner, Karl 10
laser eye surgery 23
Lavoisier, Antoine 15
leeches and blood 10
Leeuwenhoek, Antoni van 5, 10, 28, 34
Leonardo da Vinci 32
life expectancy 39
ligaments 7
Lister, Joseph 29
liver 17
lungs 11, 14–15

M
malnutrition 16
Malpighi, Marcello 11
medicine 30–31
Mendel, Gregor 35
microscopes 4, 5
Morton, William 20
motor nerves 19
mouth 17
Muller, Johannes 36
muscles 8–9

N
nervous system 8, 19
nose 26–27
nutrition 16–17

O
ophthalmoscopes 23
optic nerve 22
ovaries 36

P
pain 20
pancreas 17, 36
Pasteur, Louis 28
penicillin 31
phrenology 19
pituitary gland 36–37
plasma 10
platelets 10
preformation, theory of 34–35
Priestley, Joseph 15
pulmonary arteries 11, 13

R
rabies 31
reflex actions 21
reproduction 34–35
respiratory system 14–15
rib cage 7
rods and cones 22
Roentgen, Wilhelm 33

S
scanners 33
Scheele, Karl 15
Schwammerdamm, Jan 9
sensory nerves 19, 20–21
sex
    hormones 37
    organs 34
sick, being 27
sight 22–23
skeleton 6–7, 9
skin 21, 37, 38
skull 7, 18
smallpox 31
smell 26–27
sound 24–25
sperm 34–35
spinal cord 6, 19
stethoscopes 13
stomach 17
surgery 29, 32–33

T
taste 26–27
testicles 36
testosterone 36–37
thyroid gland 36
tissues, body 4
tongue 27
touch 20–21
tourniquets 12
transfusions, blood 10
trepanning 18

V
vaccination 31
valves 12–13
veins 11, 12
venae cavae 11, 13
vertebrates 6
Vesalius, Andreas 6
viruses 28–29
vitamins 17

W
Watson, James 35
Wells, Horace 20
witch doctors 30

X
X rays 33

© Simon & Schuster
Young Books 1994